INTEGRATED COMMUNICATIONS

Official Module Guide

2nd edition

The Chartered Institute of Marketing
Moor Hall
Cookham
Maidenhead
Berkshire
SL6 9QH
United Kingdom

www.cim.co.uk

First published 2014

Revised edition published 2016. 2nd edition published 2017

A catalogue record for this book is available from the British Library.

ISBN 978-1-907368-51-6 (paperback)
ISBN 978-1-907368-52-3 (ebook)

Typeset by Fakenham Prepress Solutions, Fakenham, Norfolk, NR21 8NN, UK

CONTENTS

3

MARKETING IS CONSTANTLY EVOLVING AND IT'S IMPORTANT TO DEMONSTRATE YOU HAVE KEPT UP-TO-DATE WITH THE LATEST DEVELOPMENTS.

Following extensive research among marketing professionals and the wider business community we launched a portfolio of award-based qualifications to reflect the market need for flexible bite-sized learning for today's professional marketer.

Each individual module can be achieved as a distinct self-contained award and, when combined with further awards, built into a full qualification if and when required.

Each module is based on our unique Professional Marketing Competency framework, which is designed to help meet the ever-increasing demands on marketers at every stage of their career.

ABOUT US

CIM (The Chartered Institute of Marketing) is the leading international professional marketing body. CIM exists to develop the marketing profession, maintain professional standards and improve the skills of marketing practitioners, enabling them to deliver exceptional results for their organisations.

Our range of professional qualifications and training programmes – along with our extensive membership benefits – are all designed to support you, develop your knowledge, enable you to grow and increase your network. Our professional pathway will help you excel and realise your full potential.

PROFESSIONAL MARKETING COMPETENCIES

The Professional Marketing Competencies are a framework that provide a guide to the skills and behaviours that are expected of professional marketers at varying levels of proficiency.

Developed from extensive research with employers and employees in marketing and other business functions, the Competencies give individuals and organisations the basis on which to assess the abilities of a capable and competent marketer.

More information about Professional Marketing Competencies can be found on our website: www.cim.co.uk/competencies.

The Professional Marketing Competencies

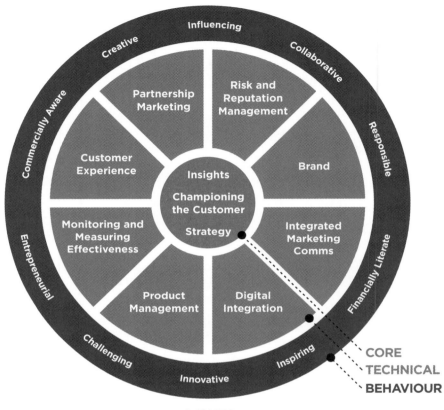

© CIM 2016

QUALIFICATION OVERVIEW

The aim of the CIM Certificate in Professional Marketing is to provide the practising marketer with relevant, contemporary marketing content to equip them for the current global landscape. Learning is brought to life through meaningful and active assessment methods, which embrace the modern marketing industry.

INTRODUCTION TO THE MODULE

Integrated communications is a mandatory module that sits within the suite of Certificate modules. To gain the CIM Certificate in Professional Marketing you need to pass this and the Marketing mandatory module, plus one elective module – either Customer Experience or Digital Marketing. However, you will gain a module award for each individual you pass.

MODULE CONTENT

This module aims to give learners an understanding of the importance of effective internal and external communications in building sustainable relationships and delivering customer value. It will help them to recognise the importance of communications planning in delivering marketing solutions, and of how product and brand management can enable organisations to deliver customer value. It outlines the components of the marketing communications mix and helps learners to understand integrated marketing communications (IMC) planning.

BENEFITS OF STUDYING THE MODULE

Communications lie at the root of all organisational activity, whether in consumer (B2C), business-to-business (B2B), not-for-profit or any other market. In this study guide we begin to examine integrated organisational communications, which includes both internal and external communications, and their vital contribution to organisational success.

New technologies and changes in communication models have meant that businesses must adapt and change as well. Marketing must take into account innovations such as Web 2.0, the proliferation of mobile devices and 'apps' (software applications), social media and user-generated content (UGC).

LEARNING OUTCOMES

The three units and six learning outcomes for this module are as follows:

1. **Internal marketing**
   - Know how to build cross-functional relationships.
   - Understand how to harness resources to deliver effective marketing solutions.

2. **Value proposition**
   - Create effective communications to deliver value to customers.
   - Understand product and brand management.

3. **Marketing communications**
   - Understand the components of the marketing communications mix.
   - Develop integrated marketing communications.

Planning the journey

You can use this workbook in the way that best suits your preferred learning style and approach to reading.

For example, you could read it from cover to cover as a course or textbook. The content within each chapter is linked and follows a logical progression.

Alternatively, you could dip into it at any point to find information and examples of key concepts and subjects. The chapters are structured around the six learning outcomes for the module and each assessment criterion is covered within the content, highlighted by sub-headings.

Each chapter contains case studies of real companies (some via YouTube links), highlighted in text boxes, which put into context the concepts and topics discussed.

There are also activities and short multiple-choice quizzes to test the knowledge you've gained while reading each chapter.

ASSESSMENTS

A variety of different assessment methodologies are used for the Certificate in Professional Marketing, depending on the module. Assessment methods used within the qualification are employer-driven, practitioner-based, relevant and appropriate for business needs.

In addition, assessments for all qualifications comply with regulatory requirements, are fit for purpose, fair, valid, reliable and manageable to ensure confidence in the standard of learner achievement.

The assessment methodology for this module is an assignment. The assessment you deliver will be 12 pages long, based on a specified scenario and an organisation of choice. It will comprise three compulsory tasks. Please refer to the module specifications on the website for more detail.

Learners are required to produce an organisation summary based on headings provided within the assignment.

OTHER RESOURCES

This study guide is one aspect of a wide range of study resources available to you in the module toolkit. No single resource is sufficient to gain a full understanding of the module content. The study guide is intended to be used in conjunction with the recommended textbook, but you will also find it valuable to refer to the further reading mentioned within the guide.

RECOMMENDED TEXTBOOK

Fill, C. and Turnbull, S. (2016) *Marketing communications: discovery, creation and conversations*. 7th edition. Harlow, Pearson.
ISBN 9781292092614

FURTHER READING

De Pelsmacker, P., Geuens, M. and Van Den Bergh, J. (2017)
Marketing communications: a European perspective. 6th edition.
Harlow, Pearson.
ISBN 9780273773221

Egan, J. (2011) *Relationship marketing: exploring relational strategies in marketing*. 4th edition. Harlow, FT/Prentice Hall.
ISBN 9780273737780

Smith, P.R. and Zook, Z. (2016) *Marketing communications: offline and online integration, engagement and analytics*. 6th edition.
London, Kogan Page.
ISBN 9780749473402

The textbooks cover the topics in this module in much more detail than this study guide – but they have not been written with the CIM's syllabus in mind. Within each chapter you will find references to the core textbook and the supplementary textbooks. To enable you to extend your knowledge, the study guide also summarises ideas and concepts from a range of key sources, many of which are available via the CIM's study website. It is always a good idea to read the original papers because they usually provide insights into a theory or case study that a brief summary is unable to do. So, the study guide provides you with an overview of the content of the module and acts as a bridge to further resources.

The case studies and practical exercises in each chapter will help you put some of the theories and frameworks into context. In preparing the assignment for this module's assessment you will need to apply a range of concepts and tools to a real organisation – so the exercises here will give you some practice and provide solutions against which to assess your answers.

MyCIM
CIM itself offers a variety of resources to all its members, including Your Study Resources, Marketing Expert, Content Hub, MyiLibrary, Ebsco and Emerald. You can find these at www.cim.co.uk within MyCIM.

My Study Resources
These are guides to help you delve deeper into material that supports the six learning outcomes in this module. The links are taken from a range of resources and direct you to the wide range of online member resources to help your learning journey.

Marketing Expert and Content Hub
Marketing Expert has a range of practical guides, templates, topic guides and legal notes on marketing. Content Hub has blogs, editorials, podcasts, webinars on the wide range of marketing topics.

MyiLibrary
The library at Moor Hall is open to all learners Monday to Friday between the hours of 9am and 5pm. For those who can't get to it, MyiLibrary, the online books collection, is a good alternative. It allows you to read a range of marketing books on your desktop, and, in some cases, you can download them to your e-reader for seven days.

Ebsco and Emerald
Ebsco is an online database of reference material that is updated every day. It includes journals, magazines, newspapers and reports covering all aspects of marketing and business from around the world. Learners also have full access to the Emerald marketing eJournal collection. An online user guide provides a detailed list of current titles and information on how to search the collection. It also contains a range of older editions that the library has subscribed to historically.

Remember, all of these are available on the CIM website.

Marketing news
Finally, one further way you can develop your knowledge and understanding is to keep up-to-date with what's going on in the real world of marketing. All members and learners can access *Catalyst,* our magazine free, but magazines such as *Campaign, Marketing Week* and *The Drum* provide a wealth of informative, insightful and fascinating information, augmented by up-to-date opinion, blogs, stories and resources on their websites. You could also follow the hundreds of publishers, marketing theorists, academics, companies, brands and agencies who post content on social media.

Or you could take advantage of *Cutting Edge,* the CIM's weekly digest of short and snappy marketing-related news items from across the sectors, available at www.cim.co.uk/cuttingedge when logged into MyCIM.

Please note: All information included in this Introduction was correct at the time of going to print. Please check the Study Connect e-newsletters for any updates or changes.

1.

INTERNAL MARKETING: BUILDING CROSS-FUNCTIONAL RELATIONSHIPS

OUTLINE

This chapter is about communication with employees. At the end of this chapter you will be able to do the following:

- Identify different types of cross-functional relationships in organisations.
- Explain the importance of internal communications.
- Outline appropriate methods for internal communications.
- Explain the relationship between collaborative working and meeting customers' needs.

The most important points to understand are the co-ordinating function marketing plays in an organisation and the role of communication within that; and the crucial role of internal marketing, where marketing, working as a service department, treats colleagues as internal customers. We discuss internal marketing in the context of integrated marketing communications further in Chapter 6.

GLOSSARY

Internal marketing – Summed up by Gummesson (2002) as follows: "The objective of internal marketing within relationship marketing is to create relationships between management and employees, and between functions. The personnel can be viewed as an internal market, and this market must be reached efficiently in order to prepare the personnel for external contacts: efficient internal marketing becomes an antecedent to efficient external marketing."

Relationship marketing – A marketing approach based on relationships rather than individual transactions. Areas in relationship marketing and integrated marketing communications "intertwine and reinforce each other." (Fill 2013)

Integrated marketing – Joined-up marketing, which is what all marketing should be.

Marketing communications – The third P (Promotion) in the 4P marketing mix of Product, Price, Promotion and Place.

Integrated marketing communications (IMC) – Joined-up marketing communications, which, again, is what all marketing communications should be.

Stakeholders – Individuals or groups who depend on an organisation to achieve their own goals and on whom, in turn, the organisation depends. Stakeholders may be:

- Internal (employees and managers).

- Connected (customers, shareholders, financiers, suppliers, channel members).
- External (communities, government, pressure groups and media).

Target audience – The group of individuals at whom marketers direct their promotional or communication messages.

Marketing environment – "The internal environment, the connected micro environment and the external macro environment." (CIM, 2012)

Integrated marketing communications are marketing communications that are co-ordinated and harmonised across channels, territories and over time, to maximise the effectiveness of marketing activities and, therefore, return on investment (ROI).

Fill (2016) defines (integrated) marketing communication as: "a process through which organisations and audiences engage with one another. Through an understanding of an audience's preferred communication environments, participants seek to develop and present messages, before evaluating and responding."

The Journal of Integrated Marketing Communication (2014) describes integrated marketing communications as: "a strategic marketing process specifically designed to ensure that all messaging and communications strategies are unified across all channels and are centred around the customer. The IMC process emphasises identifying and assessing customer prospects, tailoring messaging to customers and prospects that are both serviceable and profitable, and evaluating the success of these efforts to minimise waste and transform marketing from an expense into a profit."

INTRODUCTION

The main focus of this study guide is on how to communicate persuasively with customers – and, where required, other stakeholders. Integrated marketing communications is the modern way to do this, and it involves communicating consistent and harmonised messages at every point of contact between customers (and other stakeholders) and the brand or organisation, from the brand name, concept and packaging, through promotion, to the final delivery of the product or service.

Achieving this requires everyone in the organisation to be aligned around the same customer-oriented objectives. This first chapter examines the vital importance of communicating with internal audiences. Unless these key stakeholders are aligned with the customer-facing (external) message, this message is unlikely to be successful. This leads us on to the concept of the 'employee brand' (Fill, 2016), and the subtly different 'employer brand', which we discuss in section 1.4.

But before we get into all this, let's take a step back in order to understand how communication works.

The communications process

Most of us communicate easily and naturally, so we may not realise how complicated the process actually is. In an organisational context we have to find the most effective way to transmit ideas from one person's head into another's. Schramm (1955) suggests a simple three-component model of communication:

* **Encoding** – Designing the message to convey intended meaning.
* **Noise** – Influences that affect the quality of the original encoded message.
* **Decoding** – Interpreting the received message.

Based on Schramm, Philip Kotler (2008) depicts the communication process in the diagram below:

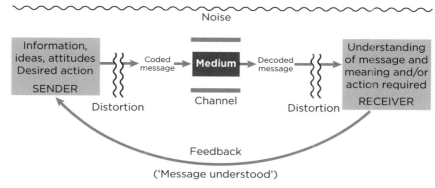

('Message understood')

Fig 1.1 The communications process *(adapted from Kotler, 2008)*

Noise – In marketing communications, the 'noise' that disturbs the reception of the message can be composed of general advertising 'clutter' or other factors, such as environmental distraction – just think about all that goes on in a typical home while the TV adverts are on. Despite the best efforts of advertisers, viewers don't pay the same attention to the commercial breaks that they do to the programmes themselves. And the problem is exacerbated by the fact that many viewers these days record programmes to watch later, and 'fast forward' through ads whenever possible. The omnipresent mobile phone is both an advertising medium *and* a form of noise: there's too much happening on it for most users to bother trying to understand commercial messages arriving by text or email.

Make a list of all the environmental distractions you can think of that could affect someone's ability to listen to and understand a radio ad for a carpet warehouse.

Encoding – This is the process of developing a message in a language that the recipient will understand and engage with. Faulty coding can cause problems: when messages are mixed, inconsistent, confused or hard to understand the recipient will just 'not get it'. An example is when advertisers try to adopt the language (and current slang) of teenagers in their advertising. Teenage language evolves so rapidly that it's almost impossible to keep up – and therefore very easy to get advertising wrong.

Decoding and the importance of feedback – The message extracted by the recipient of the (advertising) communication is sometimes called 'take-out'. It's what people actually hear (and hopefully understand and believe) as a result of the original transmitted message. Feedback from people who see ads is vitally important, because it means marketers can adjust the content where necessary. Feedback in marketing can take many forms: even complaints can be useful, and of course customers can 'vote with their pockets' (or their mouse/finger online). Marketers should ensure that they can monitor feedback from all marketing activities, including communications, in order to measure them against the results they expected or planned for. If customers haven't decoded the message as intended, it's likely to be the brand owner or agency's fault, and they should either withdraw it or change it to make it more effective.

STAKEHOLDER RELATIONSHIPS

Customers are obviously critical to a company's success. But when we are thinking about integrated communications, we need to consider a wider group of stakeholders, not least our employees (our internal audience) and people in the organisation's immediate micro environment. These groups all have a vested interest in the outcome of the firm's activities and will be affected by its results, whether they are positive or negative. We need to communicate to all our stakeholder groups so that they, in turn, can support our marketing and communication activities towards our customers.

Stakeholders are usually categorised in three groups:

- **Internal stakeholders** – Employees, casual and freelance staff, managers, board members and, in the case of charities and other not-for-profit organisations, volunteers.
- **Connected stakeholders** – Also known as primary stakeholders, these people have a contractual relationship with the organisation, and include customers, shareholders, financiers, distributors and suppliers.
- **External stakeholders** – Also known as secondary stakeholders, these people have no direct connection to the company but do have an interest in its activities. They include professional bodies, trade unions, local and national government, the media and the local community.

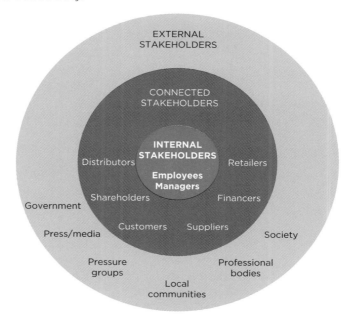

Fig 1.2 Internal and external stakeholders

These stakeholder groups align with the Six Markets Framework conceived by Payne *et al* (2005). This framework highlights an organisation's key stakeholder markets, and provides guidance on how to manage relationships more effectively with each of them through tailored communications.

The framework (see Fig 1.3 below) describes the six markets as follows:

- Internal markets (employees).
- Influence markets (eg doctors, lawyers, garage mechanics and other 'experts').
- Referral markets (opinion leaders, friends, family etc).
- Supplier and alliance markets.
- Recruitment markets.
- Customer markets.

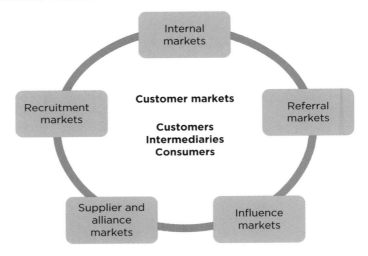

Fig 1.3 The Six Markets Framework (*Payne et al, 2005*)

Marketing acts as a co-ordinating force within an organisation, promoting and disseminating the marketing ethos, which is based around meeting customer needs, profitably (or the equivalent in non-commercial organisations). Effective internal communication helps to align everyone in the organisation behind its objectives – including the importance of 'putting customers first' – and encourages and motivates employees to look for ways to improve the customer's experience of the brand and/or service the organisation offers. An important part of marketing's role is ensuring sure that information is shared and that common goals are set based on customer outcomes and the organisation's values, vision and mission. In this sense marketing is providing a service to the rest of the organisation to help it develop and sustain a competitive advantage.

The Real Life example below shows how one large organisation uses relationship marketing to work with internal colleagues, shareholders and other external stakeholders in a seamless integrated way. The flow of influence is from the centre (that is, from employees and managers) towards 'connected' and 'external' stakeholders.

REAL LIFE 1.1

Vodafone and stakeholder engagement

Vodafone communicates with and listens to its stakeholders carefully so that it can understand their views and explain its perspectives. This allows it to address any issues as effectively as possible, and the feedback it receives informs its thinking about sustainability, which has become an important focus for the business. It tailors its engagement strategies to each stakeholder group.

- **Non-governmental organisations (NGOs)** and sustainability opinion formers are often interested in its approach to specific issues.
- **Consumers and enterprise customers** (small and large businesses and organisations) relate to it as a service provider.
- **Communities** may be concerned about the siting of network infrastructure.
- **Governments and regulators** can affect the business through new legislation and regulation.
- **Investors, employees and suppliers** are directly affected by the performance of the business.

Like all consumer-facing brands, Vodafone communicates with customers in many ways – through retail outlets, contact centres, customer research and via customer service and online and offline marketing communications. It is a major challenge (and a key responsibility of Vodafone's marketing department) to ensure these communications are consistent and complementary (see also Chapters 4, 5 and 6 of this study guide).

"Our sustainable business strategy is founded on Vodafone's commitment to responsible behaviour in everything we do.... Our approach to what we call sustainable business is to ensure that our work always delivers positive social outcomes, not just commercial and financial success. In our view, the former reinforce the latter; they are not mere 'offsets' against them. We believe in and focus on the social purpose-led approach set out in the Blueprint for Better Business, the movement established to encourage companies to act as a force for good in society that includes Vodafone as a founding supporter. (*Vodafone Group Sustainable Report* 2017)

Internal stakeholders

The marketer's role as co-ordinator of internal 'customer-oriented' communications can take various forms, depending on the needs of the organisation. In a customer-centric environment, the following will be typical priorities.

- **Common goal-setting** – there is no place for conflicting goals as result of departments working in 'silos'.
- **Freely-shared information** – customer data needs to be available for every department in a market-oriented company. A single universally-accessible database is the most efficient way of providing this.
- **A clear statement of company policy** – shared with everyone, this will determine customer satisfaction.
- **Marketing champions the customer** – both outside and inside the organisation. **Internal marketing** thus becomes an important aspect of the marketing function.

Marketing needs to be the customer's representative within the organisation, consistently looking at things from their point of view, representing them and challenging anything (in any meeting) that would appear *not* to be in their best interests. The finance director may sometimes overrule them on the grounds of cost and profitability of course.

Internal marketing – Essentially means treating the internal 'customer' in the same way that you would treat an external one, communicating the marketing and customer-orientation philosophy to them and providing services to help everyone in the organisation to become customer centric in order to foster a customer-centric culture. As with external marketing, internal marketing uses the extended 7P marketing mix to do this.

An **organisational culture** is about how an organisation behaves, and is defined in terms of shared values, traditions, symbols, stories and legends. Bower (1966) defined organisational culture as: "The way we do things around here." Organisations with customer-oriented cultures tend to be more successful. They also tend to be structured around **cross-functional teams** focused on areas such as new product development or change programmes. Such teams cut through organisational silos and hierarchies and align members behind the same goals and objectives.

ACTIVITY 1.2

Make a list of the connected stakeholders of your organisation. Are they all equally important to the organisation? Rank or score them in terms of the power and influence each has over the outcomes of the organisation's activities. How important is each one? Now consider your internal stakeholders. What are their respective functions? Do they all contribute equally towards achieving the organisation's objectives?

THE ROLE AND BENEFITS OF INTERNAL COMMUNICATIONS

As we have seen, internal marketing management is about creating, developing and maintaining a customer-oriented culture, which, together with the organisation's mission, vision and values, and supported by branding, will help the organisation to achieve its strategic goals.

Internal marketing helps to promote the 'customer first' message, engages people behind the vision ('customers are the source of profits' – or the equivalent in other sectors) and helps to improve the efficiency (doing things the right way) and effectiveness (getting the right result) of the organisation by aligning everyone behind common objectives. Digital technology – including the use of social media and customer databases – is very helpful in internal marketing, facilitating as it does the continuous flow of information through and into and out of the organisation.

The main aspects of internal marketing management include the following:

- Fostering a customer orientation throughout the organisation, including evangelising the benefits of a customer orientation.
- Clarifying corporate aims and goals.
- Providing a clear sense of purpose and direction.
- Empowering and supporting staff to take decisions related to acquiring and keeping customers.
- Recognising employees who deliver excellent service as valued internal customers.
- Adopting a partnership approach to corporate governance.
- Fostering relationships with employees that motivate them and encourage loyalty.
- Assuming that customer feedback is of interest to everyone and that everyone is involved in organisational success.

The benefits of internal marketing include the following:

- It requires leadership as well as day-to-day management, and it can help top management become aware of their own limited perspective of company activities.
- It encourages a decentralised approach to management – people understand what needs to be done without being told.
- It discourages a 'silo mentality', where different departments within an organisation work independently.
- Employees who are involved and can see the results of their efforts are prouder and more engaged, motivated and loyal.

- Greater integration creates more cohesive teams, including cross-functional teams, and helps to prevent conflict. Aims and goals are shared. This leads to process innovation and imaginative solutions to problems, which can be shared throughout the organisation.
- Marketing and other departments will improve their understanding of each other's activities and priorities.
- Improved co-ordination helps people-management processes.
- Organisation-wide customer focus leads to more satisfied customers.
- Staff who deal directly with customers are able to influence organisational policy in areas that affect their work.

A number of factors may contribute to conflict such as the reward system, uncertainty, structure or technology.

THE METHODS FOR INTERNAL COMMUNICATION

To gain strategic advantage, an organisation has to formulate and implement a value-creating strategy – that is, a comprehensive set of decisions and commitments on the direction to take in order to fully achieve its aims and goals. This process begins with a marketing audit, which has five components:

1. The marketing environment audit.
2. The marketing strategy audit.
3. The marketing organisation audit.
4. The marketing systems audit.
5. The marketing mix audit.

The findings of the audit can affect both external and internal communications.

The marketing audit has three purposes, according to Wilson and Gilligan (2004):

1. To identify the organisation's current market position.
2. To understand the opportunities and threats it faces in its environment.
3. To clarify its ability to cope with demands in its environment.

The strategy must be conceived and objectives formulated to address the issues identified in the audit. Then, subject to senior management approval, the internal marketing plan can be implemented.

The **marketing environment audit** covers the broad marketplace in which the company operates. Many factors in the macro-environment are out of the company's control – the economy, technological changes, politics other socio-cultural factors, for example.

The **marketing strategy audit** covers the following elements:

- **Mission statement** – Is this clearly stated in a functional, customer-centric way? Does it reflect the organisation's corporate and marketing objectives?
- **Marketing objectives and goals** – Are they stated clearly? Are the objectives consistent with the resources and the market situation?
- **Strategy** – The best way to evaluate strategic options is to ask 'will we reach our objectives by this route?'

REAL LIFE 1.2

Procter & Gamble's mission statement

P&G is a multinational consumer goods corporation. Its mission statement is as follows. "We will provide branded products and services of superior quality and value that improve the lives of the world's consumers, now and for generations to come. As a result, consumers will reward us with leadership sales, profit and value creation, allowing our people, our shareholders and the communities in which we live and work to prosper."

The Coca Cola company mission
This is as follows. "To refresh the world in mind, body and spirit. To inspire moments of optimism and happiness through our brands and actions. To create value and make a difference."

These mission statements, together with the companies' vision and values, help guide the organisations, and the people within them, when making decisions on strategy and brands.

In conducting **the marketing organisation audit** the McKinsey 7-S model is extremely useful because it provides a framework for analysing seven important aspects of any organisation: structure, systems, strategy, shared values, staffing, skills and style. The three following elements are particularly important in a marketing organisation context:

- **Structure** – How well is the marketing function structured? Do managers have the necessary authority and skills? What does the organisation chart tell us?
- **Systems (functional efficiency)** – How good is the flow of communication between company departments and up and down hierarchies?
- **Systems (interface efficiency)** – Are there any identifiable problems between marketing and other functions?

The marketing systems audit should cover the following elements:

- **New product development (NPD)** – Do we have a continuous and effective process for developing new products? Do we encourage staff to come up with new ideas?
- **Marketing information system (MKIS)** – How effective is the flow of marketing intelligence? Is information clear and timely for decision-making? Is it easily available to those who need it?
- **Marketing planning system** – Is the system well designed and effective? Is the system effective at forecasting sales and future trends?

The marketing mix audit looks at the following:

- **Products and services** – How does our product line compare with those of our competitors? What products should we add or withdraw?
- **Pricing** – Are the pricing objectives appropriate?
- **Distribution/place** – How effective are the various channel members?

- **Promotional mix** – Are our promotional objectives correct? Is the advertising effective? What research do we conduct before or after advertising?
- **Sales force** – Are the sales targets achievable? How effective is the sales team compared with the competition?

Factors in implementing internal marketing include the following:

- Internal customer segmentation.
- Choice of internal communication tools.
- Building supportive working relationships.
- Staff empowerment and involvement.
- Personal development and training.
- Recognition and rewards.
- Performance measures and feedback.

When implementing any change, including introducing a new customer focus, you have to expect that some people will resist it, others will welcome it and yet others may have personal objectives that are different from those of the organisation. So, as in external marketing, you have to know your audience. To help you do this you can apply the techniques of 'segmentation, targeting and positioning' (STP) to internal marketing, with segments likely to be 'supporters', 'opposers' and 'neutrals' (although different segmentation could be equally valid). We discuss the role of internal marketing in implementing and managing change more fully in Chapter 2.

The tools of internal marketing communications

These tools used in internal marketing communications are similar to those used in marketing communications in general (see Chapter 5) although the more personal media shown below are the most appropriate in this context. Employees work for your organisation, so they are already involved and, to varying degrees, engaged.

As noted above, effective internal marketing depends on the free flow of information around the organisation, and marketers should share as much as possible with all relevant parties to make them feel involved, empowered and trusted. The more employees understood the roles and motivations of their colleagues, the better able they are to work with them collaboratively.

Typical internal marketing tools are as follows:

- **Staff magazines** – These may contain similar elements to consumer 'lifestyle' magazines, such as interviews with key members of staff, and they communicate corporate news and policy in a non-didactic way.
- **Newsletters** – On bulletin boards or as desk-dropped leaflets, email attachments and so on.

- **Digital communications** – Increasingly common, these include blogs, intranets (see below)**,** dedicated web pages and the full range of social media such as Twitter, Facebook, Pinterest, Instagram, Vine and so on. New collaboration software tools include Microsoft Teams, Sharepoint, Yammer and Slack.
- **Staff meetings** – The onus is on the organisers – perhaps the marketing department together with HR – to make these as entertaining, memorable, informative and motivational as possible.
- **Team-building exercises** – 'Away-days' or afternoons where different teams can visit each other to gain mutual understanding.
- **Employee awards** – Whether 'employee of the month' or annual awards ceremonies, employees appreciate being recognised for a job well done.
- **Suggestion box** – A recognised system, whether virtual or physical, is valuable for generating new ideas from employees.
- **Video conferencing** – The growth of home-working, along with rising numbers of virtual and often multinational and geographically-dispersed teams, makes tools such as Skype, webinars and telephone conferencing essential.
- **Intranets and extranets** – These are powerful tools in stakeholder relationships, owing to their restricted access, the possibility of personalisation and the fact that they are easy to access on the move through smartphones and tablets. A restricted-access intranet is arguably the best channel for internal communication, because it allows instantaneous transfer of electronically-held information such as reports, letters, photos, videos and data, and makes the organisational address book available to everyone. An extranet extends the intranet capacity to suppliers and distributors.

Challenges for internal communications include the following:

- **Globalisation** – The workforce is more culturally and linguistically diverse.
- **Flatter structures** – More people report to the same line manager.
- **Downsizing** – Redundancies mean that the staff who remain face bigger work-loads.
- **Virtual working**.
- **The gig economy and zero-hours contracts** – The growing number of short-term contracts as apposed to permanent jobs makes people more difficult to reach.

ACTIVITY 1.3

What communication tools are currently used to communicate with staff in your organisation? How are they used and how could they be used better? Conduct some informal research among your colleagues to see what they think of current methods and their effectiveness.

WORKING COLLABORATIVELY TO MEET CUSTOMERS' NEEDS

Employee/employer branding and engagement

Engagement has become increasingly mainstream in management thinking over the past decade. There are numerous definitions, each with a different emphasis, but broadly, employee engagement brings together a range of established concepts, including job satisfaction, motivation, work effort, organisational commitment, shared purpose, energy and 'flow'. It is usually seen as an internal state of physical, mental and emotional being, but many also view it as encompassing behaviour and, in particular, loyalty, commitment and discretionary effort. It is seen to be influenced by factors including employee voice, perceived supervisor and organisational support, and self-determination or empowerment.

"Employee engagement is a useful umbrella that describes an overarching area of management strategy and has played an important role in promoting progressive management practices." (Jonny Gifford, Research Adviser, CIPD)

To engage employees organisations need to 'brand' themselves to their workforce in much the same way as they do to their customers, through things like reward, good work, support, ethical and responsible working practices, flexible working and a positive culture.

The employer brand

According to the Chartered Institute of Personnel and Development (CIPD), all organisations have an employer brand, whether consciously or unconsciously. "It's the way in which organisations differentiate themselves in the labour market, enabling them to recruit, retain and engage the right people." The CIPD defines an employer brand as: "a set of attributes and qualities, often intangible, that makes an organisation distinctive, promises a particular kind of employment experience, and appeals to those people who will thrive and perform best in its culture. A strong employer brand should connect an organisation's values, people strategy and HR policies and be linked to the company brand."

Clearly, this involves collaboration between marketing, internal communications, PR and HR.

Employee branding

This is the way employees represent the values of the company, and is the result of successful employer branding and internal marketing/communications. It's sometimes referred to as 'living the brand', and employees may be termed 'brand ambassadors'.

Fill (2016) sums it up as follows:

"The key to successful employee branding hinges upon an organisation's ability to communicate desirable values and goals, as this helps employees to identify with the organisation. This in turn prompts employees to speak positively about the organisation and so influence external stakeholders."

REAL LIFE 1.3

Virgin Trains cares for customers
Virgin Trains runs the UK West Coast main-line service. The following extract comes from its *Passenger's Charter*, which has a twin purpose: it reminds staff what the company expects from them and it acts as a sort of 'public' mission statement.

"We are committed to providing excellent customer service. Our staff are our most important asset and have the opportunity to make a positive difference to your journey. At all times we expect our staff to be smartly dressed and to respond to passengers in an efficient, considerate and courteous manner. We expect them to carry out their duties in a professional manner and to make every reasonable effort to deal effectively with customer problems on the spot. We are all aware that without you, our customers, we do not have a railway."

(West Coast Trains, 2017)

The blurring of internal and external boundaries
Increasingly, work carried out in-house is being outsourced to freelancers, contractors, temps and consultants. The so-called gig economy is adding to this trend. Some five million people in the UK are estimated to be paid on the basis of the number of 'gigs' they do - and companies such as Deliveroo and Uber are involved in legal disputes over whether the people who work for them on this basis are workers or independent contractors, a distinction that affects their rights. Zero-hours contracts are also on the rise, but workers here are at least entitled to holiday pay. The consensus is that employee brand activities should extend to these outer reaches of the workforce, but this remains a vexed issue for both organisations and workers.

Charles Handy, the management philosopher and writer, wrote about what he called 'shamrock' organisations over 20 years ago. He envisaged the workforce as divided into three parts (the shamrock leaves).

1. The core of essential executives and workers.
2. The contractual fringe, which may include individuals who once worked for the organisation but now supply services to it.
3. Consultants, under temporary contract.

Handy added a fourth 'lucky leaf', which signifies the action of customers who participate in the production and delivery of the service or product. Examples includes self-service petrol stations and self-scanning in supermarkets.

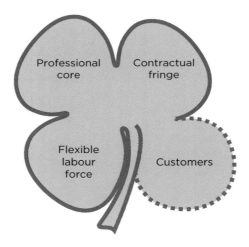

Fig 1.4 The Shamrock organisation (*Handy, 1989*)

REAL LIFE 1.4

Internal comms drive merger
The merger between Royal Dutch Shell and BG Group in 2016 created the world's largest oil and gas company. During the merger internal communications was key to maintain engagement among employees - many of whom work remotely and on shift patterns that make regular communication through traditional communication channels difficult. The internal comms team used Jive, an enterprise-wide social media platform, as a digital collaboration tool during the merger. They also used videos as a way to quickly capture messages and distribute them across platforms

and devices that were available to employees. The team were helped in this by agile leadership who were happy to create such content, often at very short notice.

See https://www.orteccommunications.com/weblog/the-importance-internal-comms-and-employer-branding-at-bg-group-during-the-merger-with-shell-interview/ for more information.

QUICK QUIZ – CHECK YOUR KNOWLEDGE

Questions
1. In Schramm's model of communication, what does 'noise' mean?
2. Which is correct?
   a. Government, distributors and press/media are all external shareholders.
   b. Government, pressure groups, press/media are all external stakeholders
   c. Government, retailers, professional bodies and customers are all external stakeholders.
3. Name three good reasons for carrying out a marketing audit.
4. Name six possible tools for internal marketing.
5. Define 'extranet'.

Answers
1. Anything that happens during the sending and receiving of a message that can disturb or alter its meaning -(eg advertising 'clutter').
2. b.
3. Wilson and Gilligan (2004) say that the marketing audit has three purposes:
   a. To identify the organisation's current market position.
   b. To understand the environmental opportunities and threats it faces.
   c. To clarify its ability to cope with environmental demands.
4. Typical internal marketing tools are as follows:
   a. Staff or house magazines.
   b. Intranet and extranet.
   c. Internal printed newsletters.
   d. Digital communication.
   e. Staff meetings
   f. Team-building exercises.
   g. Awards for employees.
   h. Suggestion box.
   i. Video conferencing.
5. Extends the intranet capacity to suppliers and distributors.

FURTHER READING

Recommended reading:
Fill, C. and Turnbull, S. (2016) *Marketing communications: discovery, creation and conversations*. 7th edition. Harlow, Pearson. ISBN 9781292092614 Chapter 9, pp311–315.

Supplementary articles:
Finney, S. and Scherrebeck-Hansen, M. (2010) Internal marketing as a change management tool: a case in rebranding. *Journal of Marketing Communications*, Vol16(5), December, pp325–344.

References
Anon (2017) Passenger's charter – Virgin Trains. *Virgin Trains*.

Anon (N.D.) Mission, vision and values. *Coca-Cola*. http://www.coca-cola.co.uk/about-us/mission-vision-and-values#

CIPD (2017) Employer brand. 28 June, *CIPD*. https://www.cipd.co.uk/knowledge/fundamentals/people/recruitment/brand-factsheet

Bower, M. (1966) "The way we do things around here": a new look at the company philosophy. *Management Review*, Vol55(5), pp4-14.

Fill, C. (2013) *Marketing communications: brands, experiences and participation*. 6th edition. Harlow, Pearson. ISBN 9780273770541

Gummesson. E. (2002) *Total relationship marketing*. 2nd edition, Oxford, Butterworth-Heinemann.

Handy, C. (1989) *Age of unreason*. Business books.

Kotler, P., Armstrong, G., Wong, V. and Saunders, J. (2008) *Principles of marketing*. 5th European Edition, Harlow, FT/Prentice Hall.

Payne, A., Ballantyne, D. and Christopher, M. (2005) A stakeholder approach to relationship marketing strategy: the development and use of the 'six markets' model. *European Journal of Marketing*, Vol39(7/8), pp855-871.

Smithson, N. (2017) Procter & Gamble Co.'s mission statement & vision statement: an analysis. *Panmore Institute*. http://panmore.com/procter-gamble-mission-statement-vision-statement-analysis

van Bakel, T. (2016) The importance of internal comms and employer branding at BG Group during the merger with Shell. 21 November, *Ortec Communications*. https://www.orteccommunications.com/weblog/the-importance-internal-comms-and-employer-branding-at-bg-group-during-the-merger-with-shell-interview/

Vodafone (2017) *Sustainable business report 2017*. Vodafone Group PLC. http://www.vodafone.com/content/dam/vodafone-images/sustainability/downloads/introduction2017.pdf#page=2

Wilson, R.M.S. and Gilligan, C. (2004) *Strategic marketing management: planning implementation and control*. 3rd edition, Abingdon, Routledge.

2.

INTERNAL MARKETING: MANAGING INTERNAL RESOURCES TO DELIVER EFFECTIVE EXTERNAL MARKETING SOLUTIONS

OUTLINE

This chapter explains how to harness resources from across the organisation to deliver the most effective external marketing solutions. At the end of this chapter you will be able to do the following:

- Assess organisational capabilities for marketing.
- Understand how to allocate internal resources to build external customer relationships.
- Understand a range of methods for setting communications budgets and measuring their impact.
- Evaluate the skills required to deliver effective marketing solutions.

35

2.1

ORGANISATIONAL CAPABILITIES FOR MARKETING

For an organisation to deliver effective marketing solutions, it needs sufficient resources and relevant empowered people.

Communications management and responsibilities

You used to be able to sum up promotion as the five classic media – TV advertising, newspapers and magazines, radio, outdoor and cinema. Some big companies even invested in a bit of PR. Today's communication landscape is much more complex, and it requires high levels of expertise and knowledge from both in-house professionals and external agencies and suppliers, backed up with the right resources, to plan and implement marketing communications in a way that delivers optimum results.

As we outlined in Chapter 1, integrated marketing communications (IMC) describes a co-ordinated, systematic approach to planning and executing a range of marketing communications activities that are consistent across all the relevant on- and offline channels.

Good internal communication is essential, but can be difficult to achieve (see Chapter 1, especially Gummesson). Its aim must be to ensure that everyone understands not only the letter of the vision and mission statements, but also the spirit that underpins them. Marketers need to share policies, objectives and marketing plans throughout the organisation, along with indications as to how they will measure success.

Communication has to flow in all directions, not just from the top down, but it's essential to secure top-level commitment to any proposed changes, new systems, new ways of working or new mindsets. Senior and middle management need to agree on and be committed to the changes if marketers are to secure the human, financial, technological and other resources they need to make marketing strategies effective.

Given the complexity of the integrated marketing communications task, including its digital and social media aspects and the internal communications dimension, it needs a dedicated professional in charge. Any marketer who accepts the challenge of IMC manager will not just be passionate about brands and marketing communication, but also have a genuine interest in people development, an understanding of how to motivate and inspire employees, and the leadership and interpersonal skills needed to work collaboratively and influence and build trust and credibility among staff at all levels.

ACTIVITY 2.1

As we've seen, there is a strong case for appointing one person to oversee all the organisation's communication. This will ensure a consistent flow of messages, both internally and externally, which will enhance the company's reputation and consolidate its competitive edge. Imagine that you have been asked to prepare an advertisement for a communication manager: describe the skills you would look for.

2.2 ALLOCATING INTERNAL RESOURCES IN ORDER TO BUILD EXTERNAL CUSTOMER RELATIONSHIPS

You can divide organisational resources into the following four areas:

1. **Physical** – manufacturing capacity, retail outlets, etc.
2. **Human** – managerial, key staff, skills mix.
3. **Financial** – net worth, capital, credit reputation, cash flow, share price.
4. **Intangible** – brands, image, market reputation and goodwill.

External marketing communication is about creating awareness, changing attitudes and ultimately motivating people to buy, and to do it successfully marketers need to harness all the organisation's resources. Initially marketing communication is aimed at generating 'trial', but it also has to build and sustain customer loyalty in order to drive 'repeat purchase' and create long-term customers who will continue to buy the company's products over time. To achieve this, businesses have moved away from transactional exchanges towards more collaborative relationships with their customers. Fig 2.1 below shows the differences.

Transactional marketing (One-way communication)	Relationship marketing (Two-way communication)
• Focus on single sale.	• Focus on customer retention.
• Focus on product features.	• Focus on product benefits.
• Short-term view.	• Long-term focus.
• Lacks customer service.	• Emphasis on customer service.
• Limited customer commitment.	• Strong commitment to customers.
• Moderate customer contact.	• High levels of customer contact.
• Quality is the concern of production.	• Quality is everyone's concern.

Fig 2.1 Transactional versus relationship marketing

The shift towards relationship marketing means that marketing communications need to be targeted at two distinct groups: prospective customers and existing customers. Communications to, and messages received by, each group will be different, but it is clear that a key role of marketing communications is to build customer loyalty.

Why is loyalty important?

Customer loyalty leads to profits. Increasing customer retention by just 5% boosts profits by 25% to 95%, according to the advisory firm Bain & Co. Brand Keys' 19th Annual Customer Loyalty Engagement Index® (CLEI) in 2015 found that the gap between what customers expect and what they believe brands are delivering is driven almost entirely by emotional values. (Reichheld, 2000)

A 2015 study by Vision Critical found that 42% of Americans will stop shopping with a brand after just two bad experiences, regardless of whether they belong to a loyalty programme or not. (Claveria, 2015)

89% of US consumers say they are loyal to brands that share their values (Wunderman, 2017).

81% of US consumers feel loyal to brands that are there when they need them, but otherwise respect their time and leave them alone (Accenture, 2017)

Customer loyalty is a deeply-held commitment that causes a customer to purchase a preferred product or service repeatedly, despite other influences and competing marketing efforts designed to encourage them to switch. Customer loyalty is important: research suggests that it is more profitable to sell to an existing customer than it is to recruit a new one. Loyalty experts say that acquiring a new customer is five times more expensive than retaining an existing one.

Loyalty programmes

Loyalty programmes are a misnomer. They may deliver valuable customer information to the marketer, but they rarely create loyalty on their own.

"True loyalty results from understanding customer needs, respecting customers, offering products that are relevant and good customer experiences that people enjoy and make them want to come back again." (Richard Kestenbaum)

"The future is all about personalisation, so building a relationship based on trust is increasingly important. If I don't trust an organisation, I don't share my data, which means they cannot personalise. So, although I think points-based loyalty programmes have their place, what we need to consider is whether they are sufficiently personalised and relevant to the customers' needs." (Jo Causon, Chief Executive of The Institute of Customer Service *In:* Anon, 2017)

However, not all 'loyalty' is good. Inertia can be a factor, as can the hassle of changing supplier. But in general, customers stay loyal and 'repeat buy' because they are happy with the 'value exchange' involved in purchasing a particular product or service. Fig 2.2 sums up how relationship marketing creates value for the organisation.

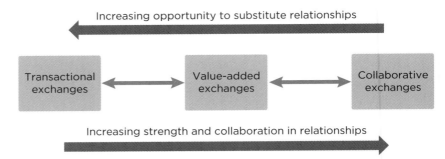

Fig 2.2 The continuum of value-orientated exchanges (*adapted from Day, 2000*)

Customer satisfaction is the extent to which the perceived performance of a product or service meets customers' expectations.

There is a strong correlation between customer satisfaction and customer loyalty – especially where customer satisfaction is very high. A customer who experiences a problem and it is dealt with well reports higher customer satisfaction than customers who don't experience problems. However, customers are more likely to leave you because they think you don't care about them than because they are dissatisfied with your service. Because customers can instantly report to millions of others either a good or a bad experience through social media, a happy returning customer can be your most effective and cheapest advertising.

Piercy (2000) categorises customers into four groups when it comes to satisfaction:

- **Satisfied stayers** – will stay with the company through thick and thin, even when logic dictates otherwise.
- **Wanderers** – are satisfied but fickle.
- **Hostages** – stay, despite being dissatisfied, through habit, inertia or supplier monopoly.
- **Dealers** – are unhappy generally, shop around and may or may not return.

However, satisfying customers is the very least marketers should aim for, and many aspire to delighting them.

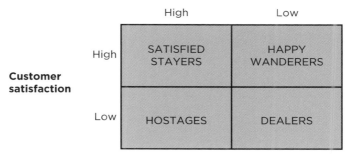

Customer loyalty

	High	Low
High	SATISFIED STAYERS	HAPPY WANDERERS
Low	HOSTAGES	DEALERS

Customer satisfaction

Fig 2.3 Customer satisfaction (*adapted from Piercy, 2000*)

LEGO, LOYALTY AND CUSTOMER SATISFACTION.

Master carpenter Ole Kirk Kristiansen started manufacturing the plastic LEGO bricks we know today in 1958. He based the name on the Danish words 'leg' and 'godt', meaning 'play' and 'well', and his motto was 'Only the best is good enough'. The twin themes of good play and quality products have underpinned the company ever since, and today it is the world's most valuable toy company and, according to Brand Finance, overtook Ferrari this year (2017) as the world's most powerful brand, helped by the LEGO Batman movie and digital innovations such as the LEGO Life social network.

A period of enthusiastic brand extension in the late 1990s meant LEGO turned its back on the brick and lost its connection with its customers. In 2004, a new chief executive, Jørgen Vig Knudstorp, got it back on track through a refocus on core products and, crucially, re-engaging with its loyal customer base (of parents as well as children).

It uses the Net Promoter Score (NPS) to build and sustain loyalty, as Conny Kalcher, VP of Consumer Experiences at LEGO Group, explains. She says that customer satisfaction scores have for many years been between 95% and 97%, but that these mean nothing. NPS works by asking children or their parents how likely they are to recommend LEGO to a friend or family member, on a scale of 0 – 10. Depending on how they score, they are either 'promoters', 'passive consumers' or 'detractors'. If you take the number of detractors from the number of promoters you get the NPS. Once LEGO has this figure it focuses on those people who didn't have a good experience and works hard to turn them into promoters – perhaps by shipping bricks to them for free, for example. "That gives you a very strong basis for sustaining your brand growth," says Kalcher. "If we turn them round they end up spending 20% more with us. If we can turn them into promoters, you can add 26% to that figure."

Being able to quantify things in financial terms helps the relationship with the finance department, she says. But "NPS is all about creating an emotional connection," which, as she says, helps build the employer brand too – the happier customers are, the happier employees are. It's a virtuous circle.

While remaining true to its original value of good-quality play, LEGO has successfully moved with the times. 'High-touch play' through traditional bricks has been complemented with 'high-tech play' through digital experiences – for example, it recently partnered with Minecraft, and its Krongiwongi Project, a Facebook campaign featuring videos of children showcasing their LEGO creations, has reached an estimated 24 million parents in 15 countries, with engagement with the LEGO Facebook page rising by over 61% during the course of the campaign. Krongiwongi is the latest in a line of efforts by LEGO to involve co-creation in its marketing strategy.

Customer relationship management (CRM) underpins customer satisfaction as, done correctly, it should ensure that each customer receives the right message, through the right channel, at the right time.

According to Fill (2013): "CRM incorporates technologies and systems that enable all employees who have an interface with customers to have real-time, up-to-date information in order to deliver high levels of customer service."

As Fill suggests, CRM is an integrated system, enabled by IT systems and methodologies, and it covers the entire business process of marketing and sales. It brings together a number of marketing and customer-facing systems within one application, and allows marketers to manage customer information and customer relationships in an organised and profitable way.

2.3 SETTING COMMUNICATIONS BUDGETS AND MEASURING THE RESULTS

As well as harnessing the appropriate human and physical resources to deliver marketing strategies that create loyal customers, you have to harness financial resources too. Managers need to know what resources are available to them, and, what's more, responsibilities are allocated and objectives formulated in financial terms. Budgeting is a vital component of strategic planning, and both are important for the following reasons.

- Planning helps to establish scenarios and contingency plans.
- Planning improves communication throughout the organisation, because plans are circulated in a timely fashion.
- Quantifying tasks and objectives in financial form helps to clarify to staff what's expected of them and motivates them to deliver it.
- Planning allows co-ordination between the activities of different departments, ensuring that everyone pulls together towards common goals.
- You can compare actual results against the plan, allowing you to make adjustments where required.

Budgeting methods

There are two main types of budgeting methods – top down and bottom up:

- **Top-down budgets** – Set by senior management, possibly with some input from the different departments, and then handed down. This is a quick and simple process, not open to dispute, and everyone knows exactly how much resource is available for each task.
- **Bottom-up budgets** – Set further down the hierarchy, submitted for approval and disseminated throughout the organisation. The process is very time-consuming and can be inaccurate because each manager, in their attempts to make life easier, tends to inflate the time needed to complete projects and exaggerate the amount of resources required.

Methods of setting a communications budget include the following:

- **The percentage of sales (or percentage of profit) method** – The budget allocated to communications activities is usually a percentage of the planned revenue. The percentage allocated will depend on marketing objectives and the level of competition in the market. In consumer markets, communications budgets are typically between 1% to 5% of expected sales.
- **The traditional spend** – The budget is round about 'what we always spend'.

- **The 'me-too' approach (or 'competitive parity')** – The budget is determined by a similar percentage of sales to competitors. (Neither this nor the previous method correspond to the organisation's current objectives, which is clearly a drawback.)
- **'All you can afford'** – The projected 'bottom line' determines everything.
- **The objective and task approach** – You calculate how much money you will need to achieve you marketing objectives and tasks. This method involves setting specific objectives, deciding what tasks need to be completed to achieve those objectives and calculating how much money it will cost to complete the tasks.
- **The share of market/share of voice (SOM/SOV) method** – Based on current and desired 'share of market' and links this with what has happened and is happening in the marketplace.

You calculate share of voice by adding up the investments all relevant competitors have made in their brand or company, and working out how much you have spent on your brand or company as a percentage of the whole. This rather rough-and-ready method of budgeting effectively means brands base their marketing communications spend on what their competitors appear to be spending, which makes no allowance for the skills of media planners, buyers or creative people in generating the best return on their clients' investment.

Organisations may decide to maintain marketing communications spending (their SOV) at a level in line with their share of the market (SOM) – or they may decide on a different level. As you can see from Fig 2.6 opposite, if your company wants to grow aggressively, you would do well to pitch your marketing communications spend (SOV) substantially higher than your share of market – maybe even twice as high. You can see why brands that need or want to grow their market share are tempted to 'buy' share by simply outspending the competition – that is, by increasing the marketing communications budget. Agencies may encourage this approach, but it is a subject on which marketing and finance directors don't always see eye-to-eye.

ACTIVITY 2.2

Financial forecasting is the heart of marketing planning. How is budgeting carried out in your company? Explain the processes used, the frequency and timescale of financial plans and the human resource involved. How could it be improved?

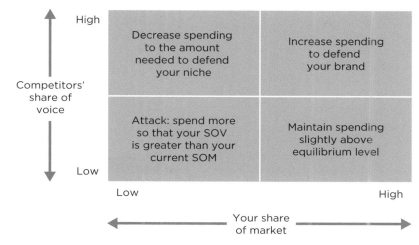

Fig 2.4 The SOV/SOM matrix (*adapted from Schroer, 1990*)

2.4 THE SKILLS REQUIRED TO DELIVER EFFECTIVE MARKETING SOLUTIONS

Marketing professionals need to demonstrate a number of behaviours in order to do their jobs efficiently and effectively and help the business to achieve its goals. It's not just what you do – your technical competencies – but, increasingly, how you do it that counts. Marketers need to be creative, commercially aware, collaborative, able to influence, inspire and, when appropriate, challenge others, they need to be entrepreneurial and financially literate, responsible and innovative.

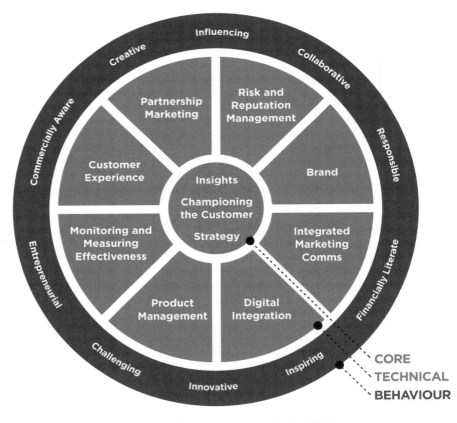

Fig 2.5 The Professional Marketing Competencies © CIM 2016

Closing the marketing skills gap

Research by the recruitment firm Hays at the end of 2016 found that companies are emphasising specific technical skills, especially digital ones, when they are recruiting marketers, at the cost of core skills such as budget management and strategic thinking, which are in short supply among new recruits. The most 'in-demand' skills were analytical ability, followed by copywriting, creativity and customer-centric thinking.

The lesson is that core skills are as important as they ever were; it is just the way the skills are applied that has changed. So while digital skill, for example, is important, people need to know how to apply it in a creative way. Arguably, marketers need increasingly to be able to combine both art and science in the way they operate.

John Rudaizky, global brand and marketing leader at EY, the professional services firm, told *Marketing Week* [Bacon, 2016] that "creativity is still king." He explained: "You can have the strongest purpose or content in the world, but if you don't express it in a simple, creative way, then people won't engage with it inside an organisation or out."

Personal skills
Some skills have become more important.

Networking is a key skill. Not necessarily social networking, but old-fashioned 'flesh pressing'. There's no substitute for meeting people face to face if you want to forge the relationships, alliances and collaborations, both inside and outside the organisation, that are essential for delivering integrated marketing solutions. Marketing is about people, and in the digital era that has often been forgotten. Indeed, the digital era makes persuading, motivating and influencing skills even more important, because you can't just push products or services on consumers – they've done their homework (online) and your pitch needs to be much cleverer as a result.

Marketing isn't a silo – and it never should have been. More than any function, its role has been to create an interface with the rest of the organisation. But turf wars still exist – not least between marketing and sales, and marketing and finance. Being prepared to cross functional boundaries – either in a new role, or as part of a cross-functional team – is essential to build your own skills and those of others in the organisation.

Networking is a great way to build your career too – because these days career paths are far from linear, and you may need to garner skills in different parts of the business, or in agencies outside the business, in order to progress. Sheryl Sandberg, COO of Facebook, has likened her career path to a 'jungle gym' – a piece of multi-level playground equipment that children can sit on, hang or climb. Networking and making lateral moves is a way of keeping your skills current – and even guarding against obsolescence. Some futurists predict that 60% of the jobs people will be doing in ten years' time haven't been invented yet.

According to the authors of 'Managing Yourself: Learn to love networking', an article in the May 2016 *Harvard Business Review*, although many people might hate the idea of networking, because they think it is exploitative and inauthentic, it is "a necessity." They write: "A mountain of research shows that professional networks lead to more job and business opportunities, broader and deeper knowledge, improved capacity to innovate, faster advancement, and greater status and authority. Building and nurturing professional relationships also improves the quality of work and increases job satisfaction."

They recommend people get over their aversion through four main strategies.

1. Focus on learning.
2. Identify common interests.
3. Think broadly about what you can give.
4. Find a higher purpose.

Coaching has been shown to be a key differentiator between effective and average managers. Effective managers create greater value for their organisations than average managers do, so it makes sense for individuals and organisations to develop this capability. A coaching approach allows managers to understand individual motivations. The most powerful motivator at work is making progress on something that is personally meaningful, and a manager therefore gets the best from their team by understanding what drives and is important to them, and making connections between this and their work. This is only possible by asking questions and exploring answers, which is a key facet of a coaching skill-set.

It's easy to build your coaching competence.

1. Listen to yourself – your language is key to understanding your current style.
2. Know your triggers – some situations will tip you instinctively into 'judging' mode, which is the antithesis of coaching.
3. Trust people to succeed and to fail – this is empowering for them.
4. Get feedback – what do your team think of your style?

Practical capabilities
Planning, writing and researching skills are essential for any marketer.

Research – For all the hype around 'big data', that on its own won't deliver the insight that marketers need in order to deliver compelling marketing solutions. There's a host of tools and websites to help marketers research their customers and prospective customers, and to learn new techniques to help them do it better.

Many people will be familiar with SurveyMonkey. Another good one is Snap Surveys, which allows you to reach people on the move through mobile devices, with lots of functionality to make self-complete surveys more engaging.

B2B and B2C companies should develop a panel, club or community of customers and/or prospects in order to build relationships and ensure good levels of participation when they need feedback. Some research companies, including omnibus providers, have developed their own panels that you can access instead.

You can keep track of developments in sentiment analysis through companies such as Hootsuite, and brain imaging work at companies such as Neuro-Insight.

You need to keep tabs on trends from a range of sectors, not just your own. Trend-watching sites such as Trend Hunter produce weekly updates that can be a great source of new ideas. Also, don't limit yourself to one approach and be aware of the limitations of different approaches. How representative are self-complete surveys, for example? And beware of relying too heavily on Google during desk research.

Writing – Crafting the right words to convey the right message through the right channel to the right audience, whether internal or external, is essential to the success of any marketing communication. Here are some tips.

1. Know your audience – and adapt content, tone and style accordingly.
2. Cut to the chase – don't bury the message.
3. Keep it simple – less is more.
4. Avoid clichés – use Plain English.
5. Avoid exclamation marks – it's like laughing at your own jokes.
6. Get active – use the active, not passive tense, and avoid ambiguity.

Practise writing up short articles on different things – not necessarily work related. Maybe after watching a film you could write a review for your colleagues, and then a different version for your boss, adapting the style as required.

Planning – Review networking events in your region and plan your approach. Do you have an 'elevator speech'? Consider what your strengths and weaknesses are in a networking arena. Check out the four main strategies above. Review what research you have as a company, and plan what else might be beneficial.

ACTIVITY 2.3

When it comes to personal skills and practical capabilities, you should consider mapping these against the Professional Marketing Competencies (https://www.cim.co.uk/more/professional-marketing-competencies/). Where you identify a skill or capability gap, think about what experience you could gain in order to plug it. You could ask to be included on a project, for example, or volunteer to help a charity or not-for-profit organisation with a project.

QUICK QUIZ – CHECK YOUR KNOWLEDGE

Questions

1. Which is correct?
   a. Transactional marketing focuses on a single sale, quality is the concern of everyone.
   b. Transactional marketing focuses on a single sale, it takes a short-term view.
   c. Transactional marketing focuses on a single sale and customer retention.
2. Define customer loyalty.
3. Explain customer relationship management (CRM).
4. Explain the SOM/SOV method of determining the promotional budget.

Answers

1. b.
2. A deeply-held commitment that causes a customer to purchase a preferred product or service and to return again and again, despite other influences and other competitive marketing efforts designed to provoke switching behaviour.
3. An integrated system, covering the entire business process of marketing and sales, facilitated by methodologies and IT systems, used to manage customer information and customer relationships in an organised and profitable way. CRM brings together a number of marketing and customer-facing systems within one application.
4. This is based on current and desired SOM and links this with what has happened and is happening in the marketplace. You calculate SOV by adding up all the investments of all relevant competitors and working out the percentage represented by your own investments.

FURTHER READING:

Fill, C. and Turnbull, S. (2016) *Marketing communications: discovery, creation and conversations*. 7th edition. Harlow, Pearson. ISBN 9781292092614 Chapter 9 pp311–315.

Supplementary article:

Hynes, G.E. (2012) Improving employees' interpersonal communication competencies: a qualitative study. *Business Communication Quarterly*, December, Vol75(4), pp466–475.

References

Accenture (2017) Seeing beyond the loyalty illusion. Accenture Strategy. https://www.accenture.com/gb-en/insight-customer-loyalty-gcpr

Anon (2016) Hays UK salary & recruiting trends 2017. Hays. https://www.hays.co.uk/cs/groups/hays_common/@uk/@content/documents/webassets/hays_1788278.pdf

Anon (2017) Ask the experts: the secrets to customer loyalty – as it happened. *The Guardian*, 25 May. https://www.theguardian.com/small-business-network/live/2017/may/18/ask-experts-secrets-customer-loyalty

Bacon, J. (2016) How brands can close the marketing skills gap. *Marketing Week*, 2 November. https://www.marketingweek.com/2016/11/02/how-brands-can-close-the-marketing-skills-gap/

Casciaro, T., Gino, F. and Kouchaki, N. (2016) Learn to love networking. *Harvard Business Review*, May, Vol94(5), pp104-107.

Andersen, C. (2016) Lego's customer experience: told brick by brick. 15 November. Relationwise. http://www.relationwise.com/blog/legos-customer-experience-told-brick-by-brick/

Claveria, K. (2015) How to keep your customer happy [Infographic and new data]. 7 July, Visioncritical. https://www.visioncritical.com/keep-customers-happy-infographic/

Day, G.S. (2000) Managing market relationships. *Journal of the Academy of Marketing Science*, Vol28(1), pp24-30.

Fill, C. (2013) *Marketing communications: brands, experiences and participation*. 6th edition. Harlow, Pearson. [ISBN 9780273770541]

Gummesson, E. (2002) *Total relationship marketing*. 2nd edition, Oxford, Butterworth-Heinemann.

Kesterbaum, R. (2016) How do you build customer loyalty? 20 December, *Forbes*. https://www.forbes.com/sites/richardkestenbaum/2016/12/20/how-do-you-build-customer-loyalty/#2ba1b5982366

Piercy, N. (2000) *Market-led strategic change*. 2nd edition, Oxford, Butterworth-Heinemann.

Schroer, J.C. (1990) Ad spending: growing market share. *Harvard Business Review*, Jan/Feb, Vol68(1), pp44–48.

Pim, K. (2016) How Lego's global empire was rebuilt brick by brick. 1 December, *The New European*. http://www.theneweuropean.co.uk/culture/how-lego-s-global-empire-was-rebuilt-brick-by-brick-1-4801533

Smith, K. (2016) The best Facebook campaigns and why they work. 4 November, Brandwatch. https://www.brandwatch.com/blog/facebook-marketing-campaigns/

Reichheld, F.F. and Schefter, P. (2000) The economics of e-loyalty. 10 July, *Harvard Business School*. http://hbswk.hbs.edu/archive/1590.html

Wunderman (2017) Wantedness. https://www.wantedness.com/

3.

THE VALUE PROPOSITION: CREATING EFFECTIVE COMMUNICATIONS

OUTLINE

This chapter provides a guide to delivering effective marketing communications that provide value to the customer, build brands and drive sales. At the end of this chapter you will be able to do the following:

- Outline communication campaign plans targeted at delivering customer value.
- Develop effective creative briefs based on knowledge of customer value.
- Demonstrate relevant messages and appeals based on identified customer responses.
- Explain processes for appointing and managing external agencies and partners.

GLOSSARY

Opinion leaders/formers – Individuals (experts, celebrities, role models, pharmacists, motoring correspondents, film critics, bloggers etc) who are perceived to be knowledgeable about a specific area and whose advice or opinion is valued by others. Family, friends and colleagues will also be amongst this group.

Marketing campaign – A series of communications intended to communicate a consistent message about a brand or group of brands in order to reach and influence the identified target audience as cost-effectively as possible.

Value proposition – A short, succinct statement of the bundle of benefits that your product or service will deliver to its target audience.

Unique selling proposition (USP) – Something that is head and shoulders above any potential competitor in terms of the benefits it offers to consumers (eg the first iPhone).

CAMPAIGN PLANNING AIMED AT DELIVERING CUSTOMER VALUE

Customer value propositions

If they are to buy a product or service, customers need to understand the value or benefits ownership can deliver. Customer perceived value (CPV) is the prospective customer's evaluation of all the benefits and costs of an offering compared with those of competitors.

The equation for 'total customer-delivered value' is the difference between the value the customer thinks they are getting, and what it costs them (in more than pure monetary terms) to get it. Fig 3.1 below illustrates the different factors involved.

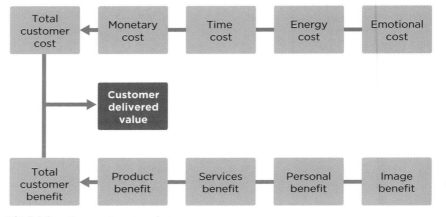

Fig 3.1 Creating customer value

Some organisations seem to have an intuitive grasp of what their target group needs or wants. But most need to find out through market research or direct feedback from customers at the point of sale, or through website surveys or in social media.

A **value proposition** is a short, succinct statement of the bundle of benefits that your product or service will deliver to its target audience. This must be very specific and focus on what your customer really wants and values. A useful approach is to place yourself in the shoes of the typical consumer and ask: "Why would I want to buy this product?"

It is very important to be single-minded in identifying the proposition for any given communication. There is a rich history behind this: Rosser Reeves of the Ted Bates agency first identified the concept of the **Unique Selling Proposition (USP)** in the early 1940s. Nowadays it is rare to have a product that is entirely unique – that is, head and shoulders above any potential competitor in terms of the benefits it offers to consumers. Examples might be the first iPod, iPhone, iPad, or iWatch. However, this is not to say that clever marketing and advertising planners can't identify benefits even of 'me-too' products and communicate these convincingly to generate demand and sales, effectively creating a USP where none exists.

You identify a USP by putting yourself in the customer's shoes:

- As a customer, what do I want or need?
- What problems do I need the product to solve?
- What do I expect from this product/service?
- What benefits do I get from it?
- Why should I choose this one over competing offers?

Once you've identified a USP you can work out how best to communicate it to your target audience. The Real Life example below shows how a USP and clever promotion can keep even a simple and long-established brand relevant and salient.

REAL LIFE 3.1

Marmite: Love it or hate it
Marmite is a sticky, dark brown food paste with a distinctive, powerful, salty flavour. It's an acquired taste – something it makes a virtue of in its advertising slogan 'Love it or hate it'. Marmite has consequently entered British English as a metaphor for something that polarises opinion.

Marmite was launched in 1902. Apart from the move from earthenware pots to the distinctive glass jars in the 1920s, nothing changed until 2002. The brand's centenary year marked the beginning of a string of innovations, starting with a special centenary jar. In 2007 it launched a successful limited edition that used yeast from the Guinness brewing process, in 2008 it released Champagne Marmite in time for Valentine's Day, with the label bearing the words 'I love you' in place of the usual logo, and for Christmas 2012 it launched a festive edition containing edible gold flecks.

In 2015 it embraced another new marketing trend when it gave consumers the chance to personalise jars with their own or someone else's name, through an ecommerce option on its Facebook page. The move was described by Philippa Atkinson, then assistant brand manager, as another example of Marmite's "innate ability to create talkability."

This talkability is evident in its highly memorable advertising too. The TV ad for the launch of the squeezable pack in 2006 showed a frustrated consumer with his broken arm in plaster, and the spoof 'political campaign' in 2010 asked people to vote for the 'Love' or 'Hate' Party (of Marmite). In 2013 the 'End Marmite Neglect' campaign, which parodied animal rescue programmes by focusing on 'neglected' jars at the back of people's cupboards, provoked over 500 complaints to the Advertising Standards Authority (ASA) but drove a 14% increase in sales within eight weeks of the campaign's launch, a wave of press attention and huge growth in its social media following.

Marmite is an old brand that has stayed relevant through continuous reinvention and clever marketing around its core value proposition of unique taste. Even people who don't like the product love engaging with the brand.

Models of communication

It's difficult to prove exactly how advertising or any other form of promotional activity actually works, in the sense of being able to calculate an exact return on investment (ROI) for any given marketing activity. But there are various models and theories that can help marketers to plan effective communication.

- **Market response models** – These measure the relationship between advertising and purchase behaviour by metrics such as sales revenue, market share and brand choice. They also examine how long the effects of advertising last. Generally, if a campaign runs for no longer than three months, the effect dissipates and disappears completely within a year. It is not enough to make the customer aware of the product or service; they also need reminding before key purchasing periods.
- **Cognitive information models** – These assume that consumers make rational decisions and that advertising provides information that helps them to differentiate and position brands based on what they know. In reality, this is usually far from the truth.
- **Affective models** – These suggest that advertising works by appealing to our emotions.
- **Conative models** – These are related to behaviour and are based on observations of how customers behave in certain given circumstances.
- **Hierarchy-of-effects models** – These models combine the cognitive and affective aspects of advertising in order to drive or influence behaviour.

The **traditional 'hierarchical' models of advertising**, referred to in the final bullet point, were based on three identified stages of customer behaviour – cognition, affect and conation (knowing, feeling and doing).

- The best known of these hierarchical models is **AIDA** (**Attention – Interest – Desire – Action**), which was initially proposed as an aid to sales people by E. St. Elmo Lewis and then developed by Strong (1925). It remains a useful basic way to look at all promotion. The premise is that advertising works by first catching the attention of the target group, then generating interest in the message, then provoking some kind of want or need and, finally, prompting purchase.

- Lavidge and Steiner (1961) improved on AIDA by adding more elements to the hierarchy, which became **Awareness – Knowledge – Liking – Preference – Conviction – Purchase**. This acknowledges that customers make choices between competitive offerings.
- McGuire (1978) formulated another model, which contained the following steps: **Presentation – Attention – Comprehension – Yielding – Retention – Behaviour**. This model focuses more on information-based decision-making.
- **DAGMAR (Defining Advertising Goals for Measured Advertising Results)** was conceived by Colley (1961). This model measures advertising effectiveness without focusing on sales alone, using additional concepts such as timescale, objectives, benchmarking and exact target audience. The DAGMAR model holds that each potential purchaser goes through four states of mind in terms of their relationship with the advertisement: **Awareness – Comprehension – Conviction – Action**, and DAGMAR is sometimes known as the **ACCA** advertising formula.

Marketers subsequently began to question whether prospects really did move sequentially through these 'hierarchies', in this order, and whether these variables were the only relevant ones. The consensus was 'not really'. Hierarchy-of-effects models can help thinking, but don't allow for the fact that the customer journey is often far from linear. The effect advertising and promotion has on consumers in general depends on many factors, including its objectives, its positioning, the type of product or service, the complexity of the purchase, the communications mix used, the company's stage of development and the target group. These factors make the effect of advertising difficult to measure and therefore to predict with any degree of accuracy.

Purchase decision-making and communications

Consumers don't choose products in a completely logical and dispassionate way. Even business-to-business (B2B) buyers are swayed by factors that have nothing to do with the cold, rational truths of 'cost' and 'solution'. The cluster of factors that make up the 'benefits' of a product or service include as many 'non-rational' as rational ones and, even in B2B markets, these include personal relationships, tradition and branding. Emotion plays a big part in customers' decisions to buy a product or service, whatever market they're in.

To shed some light on the above issues, we can turn to the thinking of the famous US advertising agency Foote, Cone and Belding, now known as FCB and part of the global Interpublic Group (IPG).

In response to questions about just how customers make purchase decisions, FCB (and, specifically, its then Senior Vice-President Richard Vaughn) produced a model based on three stages: **Experience, Affect and Cognition** (Vaughn 1986). See Fig 3.2 below.

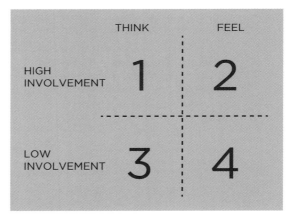

Fig 3.2 The FCB Planning Grid (*Vaughn, 1986*)

The FCB Planning Grid shows four types of decision-making:

1. Thinking/high involvement.
2. Feeling/high involvement.
3. Thinking/low involvement.
4. Feeling/low involvement.

Each type requires a different advertising approach. 'Involvement' in this context means the level of risk or concern associated with the intended purchase and how that might affect the buyer's behaviour.

- **Characteristics associated with high involvement:**
  - When consumers perceive a high level of risk (monetary or other) in an intended purchase, they are highly involved.
  - They may have developed an attitude to the purchase before committing to it, or before trying it out or experimenting with it.
  - A prolonged search for information results in product awareness, followed by the formulation of an attitude.
- **Characteristics associated with low involvement:**
  - People perceive a low level of risk in the intended purchase.
  - They seek little or no information (how many look at the ingredients on a can of beans, for example?)

- They often try something before forming an attitude about it.

By combining the elements of thinking and feeling with the level of involvement, four advertising planning strategies emerge: **Informative, Affective, Habitual**, and **Self-satisfied**.

- Quadrant 1, for example, represents **Informative.** The customer has high involvement and will seek information on which to base their decision. Examples of products that would fall into this quadrant include a car, a house and furniture.
- Quadrant 2 represents **Affective.** Purchases here are still high involvement, but are also affected by customers' feelings. Products that fall into this quadrant include perfume, clothing and gifts.

Being able to plot where particular brands or products sit on this grid can yield significant insights on which to build communications campaigns that give customers the information and reassurance they need to guide them through the purchase-decision-making process.

Vaughn went on to develop the **Learn – Feel – Do** approach, which recognises that customers can enter the purchase process at either the cognitive or affective stage depending on the type of product they are thinking about buying. Vaughn argued that the Learn – Feel – Do sequence is really a continuum, or a circular process, and that the communications strategy should be targeted at the point that consumers enter the cycle (see Fig 3.3).

Fig 3.3 The Learn – Feel – Do cycle (*Vaughn, 1986*)

Rossiter and Percy (1987) attempted to develop the FCB Grid further as they felt that it failed to account for situations where the customer moves from high to low involvement and then back to high involvement. The **Rossiter-Percy Grid (RPG)** uses 'awareness' as a necessary condition for advertising to be effective and replaces the 'think/feel' dimension with a more directly motivational one – 'informational/transformational'.

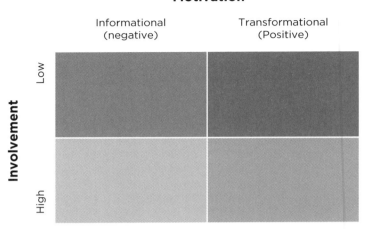

Motivation

	Informational (negative)	Transformational (Positive)

Involvement: Low / High

Fig 3.4 Rossiter-Percy Grid

The FCB and RPG Grids are essentially **models of attitude**, because they represent the way that consumers approach products or brands.

Strong and weak theories of advertising

Marketers are also concerned to know how effective advertising is likely to be in driving buyer behaviour. The **'strong'** school of advertising thinking, of which DAGMAR (see p59) is a prime example, has been dominant for many years. This holds that advertising can persuade someone to buy a product or service they have not previously purchased (trial) *and* generate loyalty to that product (repeat purchase). Jones (1991) developed the 'strong' theory of advertising **(Awareness – Interest – Desire – Action, or AIDA)**, believing that: "Advertising is capable of effecting a degree of change in the knowledge, attitudes and beliefs or behaviour of target audiences."

However, Ehrenberg (1992) countered this argument with his **'weak'** theory of advertising, which held that its role is to build familiarity and customer identification with the brand. His **Awareness – Trial – Reinforcement (ATR)** model holds that advertising can initially achieve awareness and interest for a new brand, leading to trial and repeat behaviour. For brands that consumers already know, the effect is to reinforce their knowledge.

Moments of Truth

A customer's decision to buy is often determined by 'moments of truth' – interactions between the organisation and customers, both physical and virtual. If the customer perceives they get quality and value from a moment of truth (MoT), that MoT is successful. But there are two things bear in mind: it takes 12 successful MoTs to make up for one unsuccessful one; and 'less is more' – MoTs take up the customer's time and effort and too many can be a drag on them. Organisations should aim to deliver more value to their customers with fewer moments of truth. See more here: https://www.youtube.com/watch?v=Js3CKUyrcW0

Brands and organisations need to work even harder at delivering positive moments of truth given the rise in 'showrooming' – customers in a physical store use their smartphone (and free wifi) to research a product's features and pricing, both online and in competitive retail outlets. This is clearly a major challenge for retailers, as the near-100% price transparency/visibility restricts their ability to make 'an extra margin'.

Emotional versus rational messaging – When developing the communications message we have to think about how the customer will view the purchase decision. If they are making a low involvement purchase – easy, cheap, fast – you would usually use a rational message. If the purchase is higher involvement – for instance, they are buying something important for the family – then they are more likely to respond to an emotional appeal – i.e. this is better for your family regardless of price.

The consensus is that forging an emotional attachment between your brand and its customers builds brand loyalty, whereas rational reasons are easy for competitors to copy. Many memorable advertising campaigns have succeeded by building emotional messaging into even fairly routine purchases – witness successive Hovis adverts through the years.

https://www.youtube.com/watch?v=6Mq59ykPnAE

Perceived risk – Every purchase involves some sense of perceived risk by the customer. If marketers can anticipate those and address them in their communications, they are likely to be able to speed up the purchase decision. Typical perceived risks are as follows.

Performance – Will this product meet all my expectations and live up to its promise?

Financial – Can I afford it and what might I have to go without if I buy it?

Physical – Will it fit in my house/car/office? Will it work alongside what I have already?

Social – What will my friends and peers think? Should I buy the more expensive one?

Ego – Will buying this make me feel good about myself?

Usually only one or two perceived risk factors influence a purchase and can be contained fairly easily within a message. Consider how lawyers dismiss the fear of large legal fees in encouraging people to seek injury compensation.

http://www.youtube.com/watch?v=YHbNunk0xVY

The credibility of advertising campaigns

How credible can an advertising message be when it's obvious that the company promoting it has a vested interest in the outcome? Marketers haven't always enjoyed the best reputation either: a speaker at a conference said recently: "Marketing often comes across like the guy who shows up at a party with a handful of leaflets." Marketers need to take care that their behaviour and communications mitigate these concerns. To produce credible advertising, marketers need to take into account the following factors.

To produce credible advertising, marketers need to take into account the following:

- The attractiveness of the source (likeability).
- The perceived power (authority) and expertise of the source (a dentist, a solicitor).
- The trustworthiness of the source.
- The motives of the source.

REAL LIFE 3.2

Credible versus un-credible advertising

The most credible advertising is probably a simple product reveal/demonstration in a case where there is a genuine USP. For example, the earliest TV ads for the iPad simply showed people using the product, and customers flocked in their millions to buy it. Advertising raised awareness but thereafter the product quality (and word of mouth from happy owners) did the rest.

https://www.youtube.com/watch?v=D2BvVcSkNkA

The least credible TV ads may be for products that claim to be unique or special but are very clearly copycats with little or no extra benefits over the competition. Increasingly-savvy consumers see through such 'over-claim' and reject 'hard-sell' 1960s-style communications.

Credibility depends very much on the source and the view the customer already has of the organisation. Celebrity endorsements *may* lend credibility and personality to the advertising message, but celebrities have a habit of falling from grace, which can have repercussions for the brand.

Strong brands are credible: consumers trust brands that have performed consistently over many years – think Heinz and Coca-Cola – as well as those that have performed outstandingly over a relatively short period – Apple and Google, for instance. Even in the digital era, big TV advertising campaigns can 'buy' consumers' trust and, as a result, establish credibility. However, trust and credibility are fragile commodities, particularly since the advent of social media. Bad news travels very fast these days. Just Google 'Google's bad week'.

Credibility is also subjective concept and varies depending on country, cultural considerations and the age and sophistication of the target audience. Marketers need to be sensitive to these factors when framing communications messages.

Campaign planning

A marketing campaign is a series of communications designed to convey a consistent message about a brand or group of brands in order to reach and influence the identified target audience as cost-effectively as possible. You have to 'fish where the fish are' – that is, to select the media and create the messages to communicate in each according to the identified media consumption habits and preferences of the target audience. The explosion of digital channels offers huge opportunities to reach customers and consumers, but adds to the complexity of the task.

Key inputs to this process required from brand owners and/or their agencies include the following:

- Insights into customer behaviour, wants and needs.
- Media selection.
- Effective creative ideas to generate the highest possible engagement from the target audience.

Campaign plans should include the following:

- A clear definition of the target audience.
- The specific message to be communicated.
- Desired outcomes – changed attitudes, increased awareness, leads, phone calls, mouse clicks, website traffic, store visits, sales, etc.
- Mechanisms for monitoring and controlling the campaign.
- Mechanisms to measure results.

The flow of communication can take a variety of courses:

- One-step flow – the message is communicated directly to the target audience.
- Two-step flow – the message is communicated through opinion leaders and opinion formers.

- Multi-step flow – communication flows in many directions from a variety of people within the communication networks.

Opinion leadership is important to help cut through the 'clutter' of hundreds of different commercial messages people receive (and largely ignore) every day. Despite the risks of the danger of celebrity endorsement mentioned above, expert or celebrity endorsement can make a message stand out. PR professionals have always recognised the importance of 'movers and shakers' – that is, people who, either knowingly or unknowingly, influence (often large) numbers of others. In today's world of interconnected social networks, such people wield even greater influence, and PRs are increasingly trying to identity influential bloggers and target them with brand messages – a practice known as 'blogger outreach'.

REAL LIFE 3.3

#nomakeupselfie campaign raised £8m for Cancer Research UK
On 18th March 2014 Cancer Research UK (CRUK) spotted people posting make-up free selfies online to raise awareness of cancer. They hadn't started the trend, but tweeted to say that people who wanted to do more could visit their website. The next morning visits to the website had soared, as had Twitter engagement, with people asking what more they could do to help. The charity then made its only fundraising request, posting a selfie of its science information officer holding a sign saying 'We love your #nomakeupselfie' and including a text code for donations. Within 24 hours CRUK had received £1m in donations, and began to engage to keep the viral momentum alive – providing updates on donations, thanking donors and inspiring others to participate. Within a week they had raised £8m – enough to fund ten new clinical trials.

CRUK was successful because it actively monitors socials media channels for opportunities to engage with actual and potential donors, it acted quickly, it made it easy for people to give, it sustained momentum and its 'thankyous' helped form strong bonds.

Campaign planning tools

Pickton and Broderick (2004) provide us with a comprehensive planning tool for communications campaign planning, called **RABOSTIC**. In some ways it is similar to PR Smith's SOSTAC© (2003), which helps with marketing planning, but RABOSTIC is probably more suitable for communications planning.

The model is based on two series of inputs – the planning cycle and the research and decision-making cycle that informs every element of it.

The planning cycle comprises the following elements:

- **R**esearch and analysis – To understand the market and its influences, to understand competitors, to identify problems and opportunities. Includes audience research, database analysis, purchasing trends, competitor information and results from previous communications campaigns, as well as results from research into the macro and micro environments, using a tool such as PESTELE.
- **A**udiences – Determine who to target with marketing communications.
- **B**udget – Decide how much resource you need.
- **O**bjectives – Set out what you need to achieve, who you are targeting and what behaviour you want to drive.
- **S**trategy – Develop the message and the communications strategy.
- **T**actics – To deliver the message, select the appropriate media and schedule activities.
- **I**mplementation – Put the plans into action.
- **C**ontrol – Measure and track the effectiveness of the marketing communications.

The research and decision-making cycle, which informs it at every stage, comprises:

- **A**nalysis.
- **D**ecision-making.
- **E**valuation.

Campaign objectives

Marketing communications objectives form part of an organisational hierarchy of objectives – marketing objectives cascade down from the organisational objectives, and communication objectives cascade down from marketing objectives. All objectives should be 'SMART' – Specific, Measurable, Achievable/Actionable, Relevant and Time-bound. We cover specific objectives in Chapter 6.

Typical marketing communications objectives could include the following:

- Differentiate a product or service from competing offers.
- Provide information on features and benefits.
- Create or build awareness.
- Improve the positioning of a product, or reposition it.
- Create a 'call to action' (buy now!)
- Win new business or retain customers.

Campaign strategy

As we can see from Fig 3.5, everything starts with the overarching marketing strategy, which drives the communications strategy (comprising the advertising, creative and media strategies), and, in turn, the execution of each individual campaign. Marketers should judge all proposals (from agencies, for example) against the agreed marketing strategy, which should be set out in a key document that all parties can refer to.

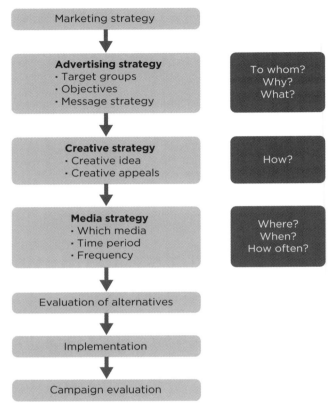

Fig 3.5 The communications strategy *(adapted from De Pelsmacker et al, 2010)*

- **Marketing strategy** – a long-term plan designed to achieve marketing objectives, and includes all aspects of the 4P marketing mix.
- **Marketing communications strategy** – a plan designed to achieve marketing communications objectives (awareness, attitude change, lead generation, clicks, sales etc).

Strategy is a crucial part of marketing planning and of marketing communications planning, although it is often neglected by marketers (and students of marketing) in the rush to get from objectives to tactics.

Fig 3.5 depicts the advertising communication strategy, but the model can be applied to each of the different marketing communications tools, including sales promotion, social media and so on. But these tools should be used in an integrated fashion, with the balance depending on the target audience and objectives to be achieved.

The **creative strategy**, sometimes referred to as the copy strategy, is at the heart of all promotional communication and delivers the tailored message. Copy strategy may include factors such as the:

- Correct 'tone of voice' to be used for particular target groups.
- Principal benefits of the brand.
- 'Reason why' or supporting evidence underpinning the benefits.
- Desired brand image.
- Positioning.

We will cover the creative strategy in more detail later in this chapter.

REAL LIFE 3.4

NHS Blood and Transplant exploits digital outdoor advertising
In May 2016 the NHS used the first ever augmented reality billboard campaign to encourage people to donate blood. NHS volunteers gave members of the public an iPhone, which used augmented reality to replicate the process of a needle going into their flesh when they hovered the iPhone over an appropriately placed sticker on their arm. The iPhone virtually 'took their blood' for 20 seconds, during which the empty blood bag on a digital advertising screen (there was one in Birmingham and one in London) 'filled up' and the real patient on the screen grew visibly healthier. A personal thank you then appeared on the screen, along with the message 'You've just seen the power of a blood donation'.

Participants were invited to register as donors. The NHS needs 200,000 new donors every year, and, in particular, African and South Asian donors, who often have rare blood types that are in particularly short supply. The campaign was focused on these groups, as well as trying to overcome people's fear of needles. Data suggests that people who see a so-called 'out of home' (OOH) campaign are 17% more likely to engage with the brand, because it's easy to do so on their mobile. The campaign was supported by social media and marked the beginning of a new approach to its marketing activity around 'the power of a blood donation' slogan, designed to raise the number of donors.

3.2

THE MEDIA STRATEGY

Media **planning** and media **buying** are different.

- **Media planning** – Is about selecting the optimal presence in the optimal channels to deliver the best ROI.
- **Media buying** – Is about skilful negotiation in order to secure the required media plan for minimal cost.

Most media agencies offer both services; some even employ hybrid media planner/buyers. Increasingly media agencies cover offline (traditional) and online (digital) planning and buying, albeit via a team of specialists in each area.

The media strategy involves decisions on media choice, the timing and duration of the campaign, its intended impact, the targeted coverage of the target audience, and the frequency with which the consumer needs to be exposed to the message. Decisions will have to be made within budget constraints, of course, but the primary consideration should be to select the media that are best able to reach the target audience and communicate the message well. Selecting the most appropriate media requires analysis of the target audience's media consumption habits – whether they are more likely to take notice of Twitter than TV, for example – and whether the message can be conveyed through audio only, visual only, or requires both.

Media selection – For each medium you plan to use you or your media planners need to take the following factors into account:

- **The size of the audience** – viewing figures, readership, circulation, for example.
- **The nature of the audience** – characteristics such as gender, geographic location, social and demographic data, psychographics.
- **The suitability of the medium's technical characteristics** for the message – for example, quality of the printing, suitability of the programming, size of text.
- **Cost-effectiveness** of the medium – cost per thousand (CPM) is the cost of reaching 1000 of your target audience and can be used to compare the effectiveness of different types of media for reaching them.
- **Measurement** – is data available to evaluate the success of the campaign?

Media planning concepts – When putting a media plan together it is important to select media that are **effective** in conveying the message and **efficient** in reaching the target audience. The **cost per thousand (CPM)** and **coverage** – the percentage of the total that a particular medium can reach – are both crucial factors to consider, but other important planning considerations include the following:

- **Impact** – the qualitative value of a message through a given medium. Often the combination of audio and visual maximises impact.
- **Circulation** – the number of copies (of newspapers, magazines etc) circulated.
- **Readership (or viewership/listenership)** – an estimate of the size of the audience, derived from market research. One issue of a magazine can have several readers.
- **Reach (coverage/penetration)** – the percentage of people in the target audience exposed to the campaign.
- **Frequency** – the number of times a member of the target market is exposed to the media vehicle (not the ad message) during a certain time period. It is measured by OTS ('opportunity to see').
- **Opportunity to see (OTS)** – although an individual may be exposed to a vehicle, they may not have seen the advert. OTS measures the opportunity. Also known as **media impressions**.
- **Duplication** – the member of the target exposed to two or more adverts carrying the same message.
- **Gross rating points (GRP)** – the measure of the total number of OTS generated in a set period. Reach x frequency = GRPs.
- **Effective frequency** – the number of times an individual needs to be exposed to an ad before it becomes effective.
- **Psychographics** – a generic term for consumers' personality traits (liberal, serious, cautious etc), beliefs and attitudes about social issues and personal interests. In a word, 'lifestyle'.

For a description of more media terms, look at http://blueonionmedia.com/glossary.php

Fig 3.6 depicts a succinct sequence of media planning.

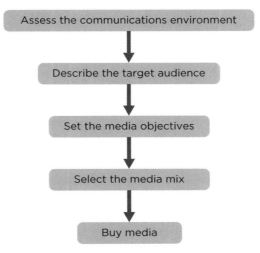

Fig 3.6 The media planning process

Media scheduling – Once the media planners have selected the media for a campaign, they will have to consider how and when to use it over time. They typically schedule the media with the highest coverage and impact at the start of the campaign to create awareness quickly, follow it up with more cost-effective media to build frequency and then, over time, adjust the frequency so as to keep costs down but retain interest. Media planners make expert decisions regarding the best use of a particular medium, but there are a number of established scheduling patterns:

- **Pulsing** – short bursts of advertising lasting days or weeks but with intervals in between.
- **Intermittent** – regular advertising but with rising and falling intensity.
- **Continuous** – a 'drip-drip-drip' type of repeat pattern.
- **Flighting** – a timing pattern in which ads are scheduled to run during intervals that are separated by periods of 'silence'. The period of time during which the ads are appearing is called a flight, and the period of absence is called a 'hiatus'. Flighting allows a brand that doesn't have enough budget to run ads (on TV, for example) continuously, to save money and maximise the impact of the commercials by airing them at key strategic times. During the hiatus it will typically employ less costly media such as radio or newspaper to keep the messages and themes of the advertising campaign front of consumers' minds.

Changing media consumption habits

The task of the media planner, in endeavouring to allocate the available budget across all available media as effectively as possible, is to reach target consumers where they consume media. This demands even more skill and attention in the digital world, which continues to reshape people's lives. It is critical that they understand consumers' media consumption habits online and offline, and how these change over time (for example, online is taking 'eyeballs' from print newspapers and consumers are moving away from desktop computers to smartphones). To do it they have to stay very close to customers and employ a range of research and monitoring tools.

According to Ofcom (2016) TV is still the most popular medium for consuming news, but its popularity is falling: 69% of adults say they watch the news on TV, compared with 78% two years ago. Just 29% get their news from newspapers (compared with 40% two years ago), 33% from the radio (it was 35% two years ago) and 48% from the internet (compared with 32% two years ago). There are significant age differences: for example, 63% of 16-34-year-olds use the internet for news, compared with 18% of those over 65, and 29% of younger people use their mobiles to get news.

According to the Office for National Statistics (ONS), nearly 42 million adults (82%) in Great Britain used the internet every day in 2016, compared to 36 million (73%) in 2013.

Seven out of every ten adults (70%) used a smartphone to access the internet 'on the go' in 2016, up from 66% a year earlier, and nearly double the number in 2011 (36%).

Other key facts include the following.

- More than 77% of all adults bought goods or services online in 2016, up from 53% in 2008.
- In Great Britain, nearly 24 million households (89%) had internet access in 2016.

The global agency Wearesocial utilises social insight to approach brand and business problems. It has a range of reports that give a global overview of the world's internet, mobile and social media usage. (https://wearesocial.com/special-reports)

Digital media provide unprecedented opportunities for marketers to get their messages across quickly and effectively, because messages can be tailored to customer segments and changed almost instantly based on consumers' response. But they also pose unprecedented challenges: the internet allows word of mouth (positive and negative) to spread like wildfire, and guerrilla and viral marketing are increasingly powerful. Consumers can compare prices, search for suppliers, make a choice and pay swiftly and easily, with next-day delivery common. But at the same time, your closest rival is but 'one click' away for a disaffected customer.

We have now reached a stage in the development of the web and mobile technology where every company needs a digital strategy, and a specific mobile strategy. Offline (traditional) communications are still highly effective, but the best marketers are working hard to integrate digital and traditional marketing to give the consumer a seamless experience at every touchpoint.

REAL LIFE 3.5

Luxury brands embrace Instagram
Luxury brands have adopted Instagram and adapted it for their own purposes. The social networking app is designed to share photos and videos from a smartphone. Given the highly visual properties of luxury brands, Instagram allows them to showcase their products through excellent photography in a way that is designed to encourage purchase – and at very low cost. Their use of Instagram also helps align them with their key group of influential followers, who are far from camera-shy.

See the link for ten inspiring campaigns.

http://bocadolobo.com/blog/lifestyle/inspiring-instagram-feeds-luxury-brands/

3.3

THE CREATIVE STRATEGY

Media planning is one part of a communications campaign; the other part is developing the message. The message has to be framed in such a way that the target group understands all aspects of what is being communicated and fully engages with it, and their propensity to do this depends on four key factors:

- The origin or source of the message.
- The balance between emotion and information.
- Structure.
- Presentation.

Successful advertising can help to do the following:

- Sell the product.
- Build awareness and brand knowledge.
- Position, reposition and differentiate the value proposition.
- Create and confirm the 'evoked set' (the group of brands that immediately spring to mind for any given product/service category).
- Encourage repeat purchase and loyalty.
- Communicate the latest information (news), especially to shareholders and other stakeholders.
- Help the advertiser to either defend the brand from competitive attacks or engage proactively with competitors.
- Provide emergency information in crisis situations.
- Build a cohesive brand story that will provide a setting for the brand values the advertiser wishes to transmit.

ACTIVITY 3.1

What ads have you seen recently (in any medium) that particularly affected you? Why was each one effective? Would you tend to favour that brand when you are in the market for that particular product category?

For inspiration look here: http://adsoftheworld.com/

Tsai (2007) has provided a model to help marketers to frame the advertising message, based on three crucial consumer characteristics:

- **Self-construal** – how the individual see him- or herself, perhaps reflected in the brand values.
- **Consumer involvement** – how involved/engaged the audience can become.
- **Product knowledge** – the individuals past history or experience.

These factors determine how they receive marketing messages and, in turn, will inform your communications approach.

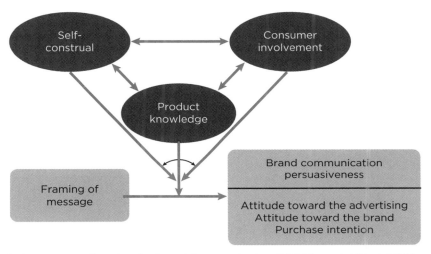

Fig 3.7 Message Framing for Brand Communication (MFBC) model (*Tsai, 2007*)

Presentation – Through clever use of print, sound and colour, advertising can dramatise the content of the message, enhancing its persuasiveness.

Content – The advertising message can tell the brand's unique story, including conveying its personality and highlighting value-adding functional, logical and emotional features. Sir John Hegarty, founding partner of Bartle Bogle Hegarty (BBH), has said: "Storytelling is probably the most powerful form of communication we have at our disposal. It has been incorporated by virtually every civilisation into their culture. It is the simplest, most memorable device we have for engaging, learning, entertaining and persuading. It's not surprising then, that so many great advertising campaigns are based around this simple device."

We looked at the relative merits of rational and emotional advertising in section 3.1, and concluded that while both have their place. Information plays an important role in advertising, but because advertising is primarily driven by the brand, with all its associations and appeal, advertising designed to appeal to people's emotions tends to be stronger.

Kevin Roberts, CEO of Saatchi and Saatchi, summed this up in *Lovemarks: The future beyond brands*' (2006): "A brand touches our emotions because it responds to our basic hopes, fears and dreams."

We look at branding more closely in Chapter 4, but at this stage it's enough to say that a brand helps to create emotions in consumers, advertising reinforces those emotions by strengthening the credibility and personality of the brand, and this can lead to enhanced trust and loyalty. Indeed, a brand's emotional appeal can be so strong that it spills over to other products – from Porsche cars to Porsche sunglasses, for example. Emotion plays an important role in this 2014 campaign from the Netherlands, around the launch of the new Porsche Macan. It was driven by a single imaginative idea: would you 'blind trade' your current car for a Porsche – any Porsche?

https://vimeo.com/88076279

The creative process

The creative process begins with the advertiser. You will have identified your precise target group and decided on your desired positioning, desired brand image and generic strategy. You can then go to the advertising agency with a complete brief for the campaign.

The creative brief – this comprises every aspect of the communications strategy, the target group, the desired positioning and brand image (see Fig 3.8), which should be pulled together into one concise but comprehensive document, ideally fitting on a single sheet of A4 paper. Creative people's time and talents are valuable, and you need to ensure you make the best possible use of them. Writing a creative brief is a skilled job, and often undervalued.

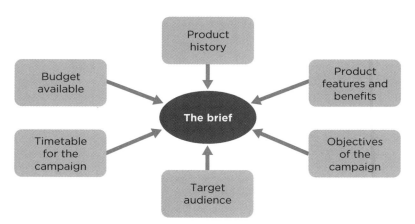

Fig 3.8 Key elements of the creative brief

Expanding on Fig 3.7, elements of the creative brief should include the following:

- History of the product or service.
- Product features and benefits.

- The target audience.
- The campaign objectives – including the metrics by which success will be measured.
- A description of direct competition and competitive offerings.
- Key information derived from market research.
- Any legal constraints – exactly what claims can and can't be made, for example.
- The budget – as a guide to which media may be chosen.
- The basic consumer benefit – USP/value proposition.
- The rationale or supporting evidence of the basic consumer benefit.

The above description fits best with consumer brands. For B2B or not-for-profit organisations, you will need to make modifications and provide additional, perhaps more technical, information.

The big creative idea – The creative team in the agency, which traditionally comprised an art director and copywriter, working together as a 'creative double', is now likely to include a web designer or other digital specialist too, along with a media specialist, and possibly a social media specialist and sales promotion specialist. This expanded team reflects the increasingly complex media landscape, and the growing need to integrate the creative message with the media used to communicate it.

The creative team will interpret the brief, looking for the 'big idea' that will become the creative concept. The 'big creative idea' is central to all good advertising. Where would *comparethemarket.com* be without the creative idea of the meerkats, which have been a surprising hit in retail markets too (witness the proliferation of cuddly toys, greeting cards and china ornaments)?

REAL LIFE 3.6

Sandy Hook Promise – 'Evan'
For a really compelling 'big idea' click on the Sandy Hook video in the link below. Only then read the commentary below.

https://www.youtube.com/watch?v=A8syQeFtBKc

The power of the film is that you don't see it coming. It's a far more compelling way for the Sandy Hook Promise to convey its message that 'gun violence is preventable if you know the signs' than lecturing young people.

For a lighter, but equally compelling alternative, watch this Channel 4 trailer for the Rio 2016 Paralympic Games.

https://www.youtube.com/watch?v=IocLkk3aYlk

ACTIVITY 3.2

We face a dilemma when briefing an advertising agency or design studio: do we give them all the data we have on a product, even negative aspects? Or is it better to keep some things confidential? Will the agency 'leak' details of what we are planning?

3.4

APPOINTING AND MANAGING ADVERTISING AGENCIES

Your agency may be part of an international network, or it may be a local creative 'hot shop'. Some companies prefer to handle their advertising in-house, and do it highly successfully – witness the clever 'Should have gone to SpecSavers' campaign, which is handled by an in-house creative team. If you use an agency, your main contact will be with an account executive, or account director. Other key people include the creative director, who heads up the creative department. The agency is likely to have a media department and research department too – although these functions may be handled by separate agencies, as might film and print production, sales promotion, PR and digital studio work.

Fig 3.9 A typical agency structure

In selecting an advertising agency to work with you will have to consider criteria such as the following.

- The agency's area of expertise – have they worked with similar organisations to yours? Are they familiar with your industry? How successful have they been?
- Are they 'full service'? Do they outsource to freelancers? How do they safeguard confidentiality?
- What work have they done for other clients?
- What is the reputation of key staff?
- Do they have experience of the media you want to use? (Digital is crucial in today's environment, and social media and web development skills essential.)
- Are their fees reasonable? Do they work on a fee basis, or could they take a results-oriented approach?

Agencies' creative track record should be a given, but marketers should be monitoring the industry on a continuous basis, through trade magazines such as *Campaign*, *Marketing Week* and *Creative Review* as well as online media such as *Ad Week* and *Brand Republic*. And while creative awards may look like navel-gazing to people outside the advertising and marketing industry, they can be a reliable guide for clients looking to identify the most creative agencies.

Going back in (UK) advertising history some of the most famous creative TV ads include the following:

- Johnnie Walker https://www.youtube.com/watch?v=h2caT4q4Nbs
- Guinness surfer https://www.youtube.com/watch?v=U3JEORDUEqc
- Cadburys Instant Smash http://youtube.com/watch?v=TBRCZLzn5pM
- Hovis https://www.youtube.com/watch?v=6Mq59ykPnAE
- Old Spice https://www.youtube.com/watch?v=owGykVbfgUE

People remember these ads primarily because they loved them. But they also meet the important criterion for any good ad – they attract attention (AIDA). They also repay that attention, delivering value/interest/entertainment as the story unfolds. However, these criteria on their own don't make for successful marketing communications: such communications must also change perceptions and increase market share. Advertising awards such as the Cannes Lions are based on all these criteria.

To see the 2017 Cannes Lions winners see the link below.

http://www.campaignlive.co.uk/article/view-grand-prix-winners-cannes-lions-2017/1437580

Communications rules and regulations

In the UK, marketing communications are controlled by both statutory and self-regulatory systems, which promote high standards through specific codes. For example, broadcast advertising, covering both TV and radio, is controlled by the Independent Broadcasting Act, but all TV and radio advertisers also have to comply with the UK Code of Broadcast Advertising (BCAP Code), while non-broadcast advertisers have to comply with the UK Code of Non-Broadcast Advertising and Direct & Promotional Marketing (CAP Code). These codes are written by the Committees of Advertising Practice (CAP) and administered by the Advertising Standards Authority (ASA).

The ASA, which is funded by an arms-length voluntary levy on the cost of advertising space, administers the Codes through a self and co-regulatory system. Non-broadcast advertising is subject to self-regulation, which means the ad industry has voluntarily established and paid for its own regulation. Co-regulation sees the ASA given responsibility on a day-to-day basis for regulating the content of broadcast (TV and radio) ads under contract from Ofcom. TV and radio ads are pre-cleared before broadcast by two clearance bodies - Clearcast for TV and Radio Centre for radio.

The ASA regulates ads across non-broadcast media, including online on companies' own websites and in social media. Its work includes acting on complaints, and proactively checking the media and taking action against misleading, harmful or offensive advertisements. The Advertising Codes require ads to be 'legal, decent, honest and truthful'.

- **Legal** – Advertising should not contain anything that breaches the law or omit anything required by law.
- **Decent** – Advertising should not contain anything likely to cause serious or widespread offence.
- **Honest** – Advertising should not exploit the credulity, lack of knowledge or inexperience of consumers.
- **Truthful** – Advertising should not mislead by inaccuracy, ambiguity, exaggeration or omission.

REAL LIFE 3.6

Wake up buddy!
Here is a campaign from Thailand that touches on some interesting ethical (and possibly legal) issues. The chain of motorway service stations, Café Amazon, positions itself to motorists in Thailand as 'the driver's buddy' with a mobile app that uses eye-tracking technology to detect signs of drowsiness. If the driver looks about to nod off, a buzzer sounds and the motorist is directed to the nearest Café Amazon for a wake-up coffee.

https://www.youtube.com/watch?v=Un5J15ilGlw

ACTIVITY 3.3

Is it safe or responsible to be encouraging drowsy motorists to get behind the wheel, confident that their Café Amazon app will ensure they avoid an accident? Would this campaign be legal in all countries?

QUICK QUIZ – CHECK YOUR KNOWLEDGE

Questions

1. What does the term 'two-step flow' mean in relation to marketing communications?
2. Explain what is meant by AIDA.
3. In campaign planning what does RABOSTIC stand for?
4. Explain the terms 'gross rating points' (GRP) and 'opportunity to see' (OTS).
5. You are preparing an advertising brief: what six elements immediately come to mind?

Answers

1. The marketing campaign message is communicated through opinion leaders and opinion formers who use their personal influence to deliver their interpretation of the message.
2. AIDA (*Attention – Interest – Desire – Action*) is one of several hierarchical advertising models initially proposed as an aid to sales people by E. St Elmo Lewis and then developed by Strong (1925).
3. A campaign planning tool (Pickton and Broderick):
   - **R**esearch and analysis
   - **A**udiences
   - **B**udget
   - **O**bjectives
   - **S**trategy
   - **T**actics
   - **I**mplementation
   - **C**ontrol
4. GRP (Gross ratings points) is the measure of the total number of OTS (Opportunity to see) generated in a set period. Reach x frequency = GRPs. Although an individual may be exposed to a vehicle, they may not have seen the advert, and OTS measures the opportunity.
5. You might think of any of the following:
   a. The history of the product or service.
   b. Product features and benefits.
   c. The target audience.
   d. The campaign objectives, including the metrics to measure success.
   e. A description of direct competition and competitive offerings.
   f. Key information derived from market research.
   g. Any legal constraints, for example, about exactly what claims can be made.
   h. The budget.
   i. The basic consumer benefit – USP/value proposition.
   j. The rationale or supporting evidence of the basic consumer benefit.

FURTHER READING

Fill, C. and Turnbull, S. (2016) *Marketing communications: discovery, creation and conversations*. 7th edition. Harlow, Pearson. ISBN 9781292092614 Chapter 7 pp211–251 and Chapter 17 pp546–586.

References

Anon (n.d.) Glossary of advertising/media terms. Blue Onion Media. http://blueonionmedia.com/glossary.php

Anon (n.d.) Ads of the world. http://adsoftheworld.com/

Anon (n.d.) Porsche blind trade. https://vimeo.com/88076279

Anon (2017) Digital in 2017: Global overview. Wearsocial. https://wearesocial.com/special-reports

Colley, R.H. (1961) *Defining advertising goals*. New York, Association of National Advertisers.

De Pelsmacker, P., Geuens, M. and Van den Bergh, J. (2010) *Marketing communications: a European perspective*. 4th edition. Harlow, Prentice Hall.

Ehrenberg, A.S.C (1992) Comments on how advertising works. *Marketing and Research Today*, August, pp167–169.

Jeary, K. (2014) Discovering the right voice for the brand. *Fourth Source*, 29 August. http://www.fourthsource.com/general/discovering-right-voice-brand-17715

Jones, J.P. (1991) Over-promise and under-deliver. *Marketing and Research Today*, November, pp192–203.

Kiefer, B. (2017) View all the Grand Prix winners from Cannes Lions 2017. Campaignlive.co.uk. (registration required) http://www.campaignlive.co.uk/article/view-grand-prix-winners-cannes-lions-2017/1437580

Lavidge, R.J. and Steiner, G.A. (1961) A model for predictive measurements of advertising effectiveness. *Journal of Marketing*, October, Vol25(6), pp59–62.

McGuire, W.J. (1978) An information-processing model of advertising effectiveness. *In: Behavioural management science in marketing* (eds) Favis, H.L and Silk, A.I., New York, Ronald Press, pp156–180.

Ofcom (2016) *The communications market 2016*. Ofcom. https://www.ofcom.org.uk/research-and-data/multi-sector-research/cmr/cmr16

ONS (2016) Internet access – households and individuals. ONS https://www.ons.gov.uk/peoplepopulationandcommunity/householdcharacteristics/homeinternetandsocialmediausage/bulletins/internetaccesshouseholdsandindividuals/2016

Pickton, D. and Broderick, A. (2004) *Integrated marketing communications*. 2nd edition, Harlow, Prentice Hall.

Reeves, R. (1961) Reality in advertising. https://prot-adar8-5773.s3.amazonaws.com/Reality-In-Advertising.pdf

Roberts, K. (2006) *Lovemarks: the future beyond brands*. Powerhouse books.

Rossiter, J.R. and Percy, L. (1997) *Advertising communication and promotion management*. 2nd ed. New York, McGraw-Hill.

Shaw, A. (2011) Involvement and motivational advertising strategies. 30 November, Strategic Planet. http://www.strategic-planet.com/2011/11/involvement-and-motivational-advertising-strategies/

Smith, P.R. (2003) SOSTAC ®. http://prsmith.org/sostac/

St. Elmo Lewis, E. (1903) Catch-line and argument. *The Book-Keeper*, February, Vol15, p124.

Strong, E.K. (1925) Theories of selling. *Journal of Applied Psychology*, Vol9, pp75–86.

Tsai, S-P. (2007) Message framing for strategy for brand communication. *Journal of Advertising Research*, September, pp365–377.

Vaughn, R. (1986) How advertising works: a planning model revisited. *Journal of Advertising Research*, Feb/Mar, Vol26(1), pp57–66.

Winston, H. 10 inspiring Instagram feeds from top luxury brands. Boco do Lobo. http://bocadolobo.com/blog/lifestyle/inspiring-instagram-feeds-luxury-brands/

You Tube
Injury Laywers 4U – women lawyer falls over (2011) YouTube, 2 October, Steveh31 http://www.youtube.com/watch?v=YHbNunk0xVY

What is iPad? – New Apple TV commercial + FAQ.(2010) YouTube video, 14 May, Tech Australia. https://www.youtube.com/watch?v=D2BvVcSkNkA

Guinness 'surfer' (2008) Youtube video, 11 December, DigitalCinemaMedia https://www.youtube.com/watch?v=U3JEORDUEqc

Hovis 'bike' advert 1973 (2007) YouTube video, 30 June, carltonreid https://www.youtube.com/watch?v=6Mq59ykPnAE

Johnnie Walker – Dear Brother (2015) YouTube video, 14 December, Doran & Daniel https://www.youtube.com/watch?v=h2caT4q4Nbs

Old Spice | The man your man could smell like (2010) YouTube video, 4 February, Old Spice. https://www.youtube.com/watch?v=owGykVbfgUE

Café Amazon: "Drive awake" application. (2013) YouTube video, 10 May, Anuway Nitipanont. https://www.youtube.com/watch?v=Un5J15ilGlw

Moments of Truth – moments that matter (2015) YouTube video, 6 March, Future Smith. https://www.youtube.com/watch?v=Js3CKUyrcW0

Evan (2016) YouTube video, 2 December, Sandy Hook Promise https://www.youtube.com/watch?v=A8syQeFtBKc

We're The Superhumans | Rio Paralympics 2016 Trailer (2016) YouTube video, 14 July, Channel 4 https://www.youtube.com/watch?v=IocLkk3aYlk

Classic Cadbury's Smash 1970 TV advert (2012) YouTube video, 22 September, tommymobile1 http://youtube.com/watch?v=TBRCZLzn5pM

4.

THE VALUE PROPOSITION: UNDERSTANDING PRODUCT AND BRAND MANAGEMENT

OUTLINE

This chapter is all about brands – how they are created, what they stand for and how they can be maintained and strengthened to deliver long-term returns for their owners. At the end of this chapter you will be able to:

- Define the concept of product management.
- Explain the concepts of brands and branding.
- Discuss the benefits of branding.
- Explain methods of building brands.

GLOSSARY

A **product** is "a physical good, service, idea, person or place that is capable of offering tangible and intangible attributes that individuals or organisations regard as so necessary, worthwhile or satisfying that they are prepared to exchange money, patronage or some other unit of value in order to acquire it." (Brassington and Pettitt, 2006).

A **brand** is "a name or symbol which identifies a product. A successful brand identifies a product as having a sustainable, competitive advantage." (McDonald and Wilson, 2011).

Brand equity is "a set of assets linked to a brand's name and symbol that adds to the value provided by a product or service to a firm and that firm's customers." (Aaker, 1991).

4.1

Product categories and classes

A product, or a service, is a 'package' of benefits that satisfies a set of consumer wants or needs. Products can be:

- **Tangible** – for example, food and drink, household appliances, cars.
- **Intangible** – for example, a holiday, pension plan, home contents insurance.
- **Service** – provided by, for example, an advertising agency, accountancy firm, beauty parlours.

Goods are often classified based on consumers' purchase behaviour:

- **Shopping goods** – for example, groceries such as tinned food or fruit and vegetables, toothpaste, detergent, hardware, fashion
- **Convenience goods** – such as ready-made meals, pizzas and frozen TV dinners.
- **Speciality goods** – specific brands that customers go out of their way to purchase. A speciality shop is one where only very specific items are sold – mobile phones and tablet computers, for example.
- **Fashion goods** – clothes, shoes and accessories.
- **Unsought goods** – the most difficult category to advertise and sell, because most people would prefer not to have to buy them. Examples include life insurance, funeral services and fire extinguishers. Certain products within this category are also known as 'distress purchases'.

Organisational purchases can be classified as:

- Installations – phone systems, printing machine.
- Accessories – satellite navigation systems, shelving units.
- Raw materials – flour, oil, steel.
- Components – wheels, semiconductors.
- Supplies – stationery, printer ink.

Product management

The product (or brand) manager is normally responsible for maintaining and adjusting the 7P marketing mix. This is typically an operational role, not a strategic one. The following are some of the areas in which he or she will operate:

- Anticipating and developing latent demand. Latent demand is a desire or preference that a consumer can't satisfy either because they don't know about relevant products, there are no relevant products, or they lack money. One of marketing's key objectives is to influence the prospective buyer to allocate his or her available money in favour of the marketer's own products and services. To do this the marketer has to convince the potential buyer of the value of the proposed transaction.

- Keeping the marketing plan on track, making sure that objectives are met.
- Maintaining and updating information on target audiences.
- Trend analysis – of the product or service and the competitive set.
- Managing the client-agency relationship.

The anatomy of a product

A product has different elements to it, even before it becomes a 'brand', as Fig 4.1 shows:

- **Core product** – the basic benefit that all products in a particular group have. For example, all cars are forms of transport.
- **Actual product** – includes the features required to access the core benefit. A car has an engine and a steering wheel, for example, and toothpaste has a tube.
- **Extended/augmented product** – includes extra features, which differentiate one product from another. A car will have a certain level of after-sales service, or a warranty, for example.
- **Potential product** – all the product could be. Driverless cars will be trialled this year (2017), for example.

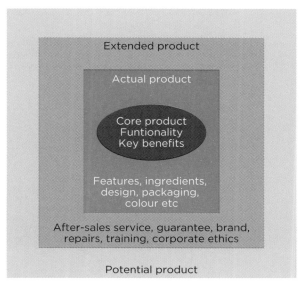

Fig 4.1 Aspects of a product

Product features, use and benefits

- **Features** – these differentiate the product apart from the competition – for example, Red Bull gives you energy, Audi offers 'Vorsprung durch Technnik'.
- **Use** – you can create a position in buyers' minds by telling them when and how a product can be used – Wash and Go shampoo, or After Eight mints, for example.
- **Benefits** – you can also create a position by setting out the benefits that users will get from a product or service. Sensodyne toothpaste, Direct Line insurance and SMART cars are examples.
- **Development** – the company is typically investing and earning no income.
- **Introduction** – revenue may grow slowly and the company may still be making a loss.
- **Growth** – the spurt phase of rapid growth.
- **Maturity** – or 'saturation', where growth is minimal or non-existent.
- **Decline** – a short-term recovery may be possible.
- **Obsolescence** – or phasing out.

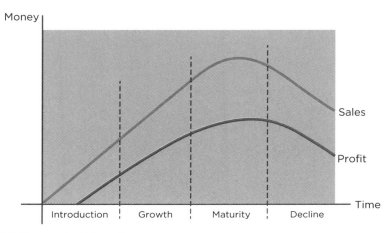

Fig 4.2 The product lifecycle

Almost all products and services follow the product lifecycle curve. During the decline phase, some will enjoy regular revivals (children's toys such as the hula-hoop and the yo-yo are often cited as examples), while others disappear shortly after they are introduced. You can apply product lifecycle strategies to different categories of products and services, and even industries, but you should use it only as a guide, given the following caveats.

- It can be difficult to determine what stage a product is in or predict how long each stage will last.
- The time a product will spend in any stage is too unpredictable to use as a basis for forecasting.
- Not all brands become obsolete – some have existed for over 100 years.
- The theory over-emphasises new product development (NPD) at the expense of mature products.

New product development

As products become obsolete, you can substitute them with new products in order to keep customers satisfied. NPD is risky (it is costly and has a high failure rate) but essential – it ensures that the organisation is never standing still. NPD allows you to refresh or extend the range, adapt to environmental opportunities and threats and give consumers 'new' news, all of which contribute to a successful long-term business strategy.

A product may be categorised as 'new' if it meets any of the following criteria:

- 'New to the world'.
- Introduced into a new market.
- Is a substitute for another product – sweetener rather than sugar, for example.
- Broadens the market for an existing product – Lucozade was originally a convalescent drink but was redeveloped as a sports drink.
- The packaging is changed significantly (therefore a new form of delivery) – for example coffee capsules and 'pods'.
- A new marketing approach is used (repositioning).

REAL LIFE 4.2

Apple Watch creates a new category
Apple Watch, launched in 2015, is a wrist computer, a health and fitness tracker, a notification system, a remote control a communicator – and a watch – all bound up in one wearable product. Another category-creating innovation from Apple, it was the first major new product category launched under Tim Cook, Steve Jobs' successor as CEO. Marketing focused on it as a fashion

accessory, and played down the technological aspects – there was a 12-page advertising spread in an issue of *Vogue*, for example. Since late 2016 Apple has been offering two versions. Series 2 includes a brighter display and GPS, and is swim-proof. Apple has sold over 25 million watches, making it the most successful wearable device ever.

https://www.youtube.com/watch?v=BoPHWtoHWqc&t=28s

The process of NPD is generally follows the process outlined in Fig 4.3.

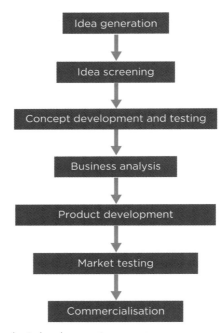

Fig 4.3 The new product development process

- **Idea generation** – Many companies encourage their employees to come up constantly with new ideas, whether relating to processes, modifications or completely new products and services. Customers can also be a source of new product ideas. Techniques such as brainstorming, attribute listing and problem analysis can generate ideas.
- **Idea screening** – You need to filter ideas in order to eliminate those that are unlikely to succeed. Screening should include questions such as: is this idea technically feasible, is it truly of benefit to customers, can we deliver it for a reasonable price at a profit?

- **Concept development and testing** – In order to test new products you need to make an experimental prototype, or a small batch of them. This allows you to study and perfect production techniques and provides a model to test with consumers. At this stage marketing will want to produce packaging or even a storyboard to test the marketing concept.
- **Business analysis** – You have to draw up a business case for the board for each new product you want to develop, including a full description of the product and its benefits, the target audience, costs estimates, sales forecasts, ROI and market share.
- **Product development** – This is the stage where you produce working prototypes or batches. You can provide samples for home testing, or for testing in a retail environment, and use the results to iron out glitches. You should define the marketing mix for the product at this stage.
- **Full scale market testing** – At this stage – and hopefully not before – the competition will finally become aware of what you're doing and you can gauge public reaction. Some companies are tempted to skip this step, for cost or speed-to-market reasons, but it does allow you to make adjustments to the marketing mix.

REAL LIFE 4.3

Shell and Ferrari

Shell's technical partnership with Scuderia Ferrari in Formula 1 dates back to the inaugural F1 season in 1950. It's one of the longest-running and most successful partnerships in F1 history: the team has won 12 Drivers titles and ten Constructors' titles powered and protected by Shell's race fuel and lubricant. Even before F1 started, the first race car Enzo Ferrari drove in 1929 was filled with Shell fuels. The two companies recently elevated their relationship to an Innovation Partnership, in which Shell will continue to power the racing teams in F1 and Scuderia Ferrari (the racing team division of the Ferrari marque) will support Shell's global Eco-marathon programme, which challenges young engineers from around the world to design, build and drive energy-efficient vehicles.

Ferrari says that Shell's products account for 25% of the team's performance gain – amounting to 30 seconds over a race distance. The benefits flow both ways: being able to test its products in the F1 arena lends Shell both technical and brand edge. The Shell V-Power race fuel used by Scuderia Ferrari contains 99% of the same types of compounds as found in Shell V-Power Unleaded road fuels available to customers worldwide.

Shell technicians and Ferrari engineers work together in each others' facilities and laboratories, and Shell shares the story of its 'Track to Road' fuel and lubricant development programme with customers and other stakeholders around the world. There is clear brand alignment: both companies share a passion for excellent performance.

This year (2017) Shell joins Ferrari in celebrating its 70th anniversary as manufacturer of what are arguably the world's most charismatic and desirable cars.

(*Shell, 2017*)

Shell is at the cutting-edge of engine fuel and lubricant technology, as the Real Life example above illustrates. Today's consumers are increasingly sceptical about the superiority of one band of petrol (gasoline) over another. While the oil companies continue to promote products that promise to 'care for your engine' or offer 'super fuel efficiency', most consumers regard petrol as a 'commodity' (that is, there is no functional difference between different brands) and consequently buy based on price and/or convenience. Shell's relationship with Scuderia Ferrari, therefore, lends it invaluable reputational edge.

https://www.youtube.com/watch?v=pRPMdY6hg50

BRANDS AND BRANDING

Organisations produce products or provide services, but customers buy and engage with brands. Therefore, successful brand-building is arguably the biggest challenge that marketers face. A brand is a product or service that carries lots of positive associations in customers' heads, based on its quality, consistency and values. Someone once described a brand as being like a familiar face at a party – it stands out from the crowd. The brand, whether corporate or product/service, is the foundation of all marketing communication. The primary role of marketing is to generate brand awareness and create, maintain and strengthen brand image, because strong brands, which are trusted by customers, produce strong profits.

You can categorise brands in different ways:

- **FMCG (fast-moving consumer goods)** – The classic area for brands and marketing. Typical examples include Dove soap, Heinz soup, Daz detergent, Colgate toothpaste.
- **Service brands** – HSBC bank, Admiral insurance.
- **B2B brands** – Hilti, Intel.
- **Professional services brands** – Ernst and Young, McKinsey.
- **Entertainment brands** – Manchester United, Sky.
- **Not-for-profit brands** – Oxfam, the BBC.
- **Corporate brands** – Coca-Cola, Marks and Spencer.

The American Marketing Association (AMA) defines a brand as: "a name, term, sign, symbol or design, or a combination of them, intended to identify the goods and services of one seller or group of sellers and to differentiate them from those of the competition."

Keller (2008) describes a brand as: "...something that has actually created a certain amount of awareness, reputation (and) prominence... in the marketplace."

Until a few decades ago, only manufacturers had brands, but as the big supermarket chains became more powerful they started to create their own brands too. Tesco, Waitrose and Marks and Spencer all have their own brands, and have created sub-brands, including 'value brands', which compete with chains such as Aldi and Lidl, whose value proposition stole share from the main players during and after the recession. Tesco 'Value' and Waitrose 'Essentials' ranges are examples.

Customers make purchase decisions based on their perception of value, and advertising can influence these perceptions. Shoppers on a tight budget may feel they have no option but to buy the cheapest available. Others may shop at Aldi and Lidl because they feel it is a smart choice – they are buying quality products without fancy labels. Others choose to shop at Waitrose, Selfridges or Harrods Food Hall because they love the brands, can afford to pay a premium and may even be motivated by their 'snob' value.

EXPLAIN THE CONCEPTS OF BRANDS AND BRANDING

Many different elements go into building a successful brand, and many marketers get confused between them. Here's a quick guide to some of the main ones.

Brand identity, or '**brand vision**', is the cornerstone of brand strategy and brand building. It is basically what you want the brand to stand for in the eyes of customers, employees and other stakeholders. Brand expert David Aaker (Aaker, 2014) prefers 'vision' to 'identity' because "it better captures the strategic, aspirational nature of the concept." 'Identity' has less energy and may be confused with the logo and visual identity.

Marketers have to find two to five compelling 'core vision elements', which will be reflected in the brand value propositions and drive brand building. A brand vision is likely to be aspirational and may or may not encapsulate the brand essence. The vision of the Hitachi Group, which has started building trains in the UK, is, for example, Inspire the Next.

Brand values should be evident in every touchpoint and communication between the brand and its stakeholders – including its employees. Shared values can shape a behavioural framework that enables an organisation to achieve its vision. In an uncertain and confusing world, consumers, employees and other stakeholders are increasingly interested in buying, working for/on, investing in, etc, brands whose beliefs and principles are aligned with their own.

When establishing brand values ask yourself:

- Are they authentic and memorable?
- Do they differentiate the brand?
- Do they encourage measurable behaviour that will enhance the brand's performance?

Brand values can help inform the brand personality and the brand promise.

Brand promise or proposition – This is the emotional and rational benefits that customers derive from purchasing the product or service. Neither advertising nor any other form of communication will deliver value unless the brand promise or proposition is clear. Apple's proposition, for example, is around exciting new products and an exemplary user experience, while BMW's centres on a great driving experience combined with environmental responsibility.

Brand personality, differentiation and positioning – A brand's personality reflects one or a number of human characteristics that consumers can relate to. The toiletries brand Dove, for example, uses 'sincerity'. Sincerity is one of five main types of brand personality identified by Jennifer Aaker (see Brand models below), the others being excitement, ruggedness, competence and sophistication. Customers are more likely to purchase a brand if its personality is similar to their own. A brand's personality helps to position it in the marketplace and differentiate it from other, ostensibly similar, brands. We discuss positioning and repositioning in section 4.4

Brand image – The impression in the consumer's mind of a brand's total personality, comprising actual and perceived qualities and shortcomings. In a sense, this is the one element of branding that the organisation can't control, because it exists in the consumer's mind. However, they can influence it through advertising campaigns and by ensuring that consumers' and other stakeholders' experience of it is consistently positive.

4.3

BENEFITS OF BRANDING

Aaker (1991) defined brand equity as: "a set of assets linked to a brand's name and symbol that adds to the value provided by a product or service to a firm and that firm's customers."

Major brand asset categories include the following:

- Brand name awareness.
- Brand loyalty.
- Perceived quality.
- Brand associations.

John Stuart, CEO of Quaker Oats between 1922-1953, was well aware of the value of brands almost a century ago. He said: "If this business were to be split up, I would take the brands, trademarks and goodwill. You could have all the bricks and mortar. And I know I would fare better than you".

Benefits of a strong brand include the following:

- Improved perceptions of value.
- Trust.
- Less vulnerability to competition
- Less vulnerability to crises.
- Larger margins.
- More inelastic response to price increases.
- Platform for brand extensions.
- Possible licensing opportunities

ACTIVITY 4.1

Distinguish between brand vision and brand image.

Brand loyalty

There are degrees of loyalty:

1. Top of mind or brand recognition.
2. Brand preference.
3. The customer will not accept substitutes.

The model most referred to when discussing customer loyalty is the Ladder of Loyalty (Christopher *et al*, 2002).

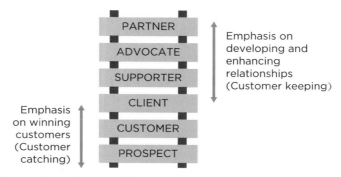

Fig 4.4 The Ladder of Loyalty (*Christopher et al, 2002*)

As Fig 4.4 shows, the model visualises the relationship with customers in terms of climbing an imaginary ladder. Marketing's task is to move potential customers up successive rungs through building brands and relationship marketing, to the point where they become not just advocates, and support you through endorsements, recommendations and referrals, but also partners, who play an active part in creating value for your organisation.

To help them do this, marketers need the full support of everyone within the organisation, and will use internal marketing and employee branding techniques, as discussed in Chapter 1, to motivate and inspire all employees to help to build and sustain strong brands. Employees have to 'live the brand', (the concept of 'employee branding'), and we all know companies where this happens – staff are friendly and helpful – and companies where it doesn't. Marketers should aspire to create positive cultures, which requires attention-to-detail in recruitment, training, remuneration policies and, crucially, internal communications.

Brand valuation

The power of brands is evident from the annual league tables of top global brands, run by companies including Interbrand and Millward Brown. Millward Brown's BrandZ™ 2017 ranking of the world's 100 most valuable brands puts Google at the top, with a brand value of over $245 billion, followed by Apple, at nearly $235 billion, and Microsoft, at over $143 billion. Technology brands dominate the table, with more traditional global brand powerhouses such as McDonald's and Coca-Cola relegated to sixth and ninth place, with values of $115 billion and $102 billion respectively.

Marketers who build strong brands can build customer preference and competitive advantage, creating a return on investment from their marketing activities and an increase in value for the whole organisation. The value that resides in the brand – whether product or service brands, or the corporate brand – is called **brand equity**. Because brand value drives competitive advantage it's important to measure it, and a whole industry exists to help marketers do this.

However, there is no single approach to measuring brand equity, as it involves measuring intangible elements that can be difficult to define. Even the specialist consultancies, such as Interbrand and Brand Finance, use different methodologies – which can result in different valuations of the same brand. However, it's not so much the absolute value that is important for marketers – though they love to see their organisations ranking high in the league tables – but rather an understanding of the elements that make up that value, and how to build on those to create more value.

Indeed, it is the 'evaluation' rather than 'valuation' that's important – all the diagnostic work that goes on to determine how healthy brands actually are. Companies can find, for example, that the brands they love don't deliver much return, but the brands they pay little attention to are potential goldmines. The old adage 'you manage what you measure' is as true in brand valuation as anywhere: you can unlock far greater value from your brands by managing them better.

Brands on the balance sheet

The debate about whether or not brands should be reflected on company balance sheets has rumbled on for many years. Intangibles, including brands, are estimated to account for around 75% of a company's worth, and growing. But accounting practice doesn't reflect this. You have to list acquired goodwill (intangibles, including brands) on the balance sheet, after an acquisition, for example, but you can't list homegrown brands. And you can only list acquired brands at the acquisition price – despite the rise in value that your new ownership ought to have created.

Listing brands on the balance sheet bolsters its value, making it easier and cheaper to borrow money and helping defend the company against takeover bids. Ranks Hovis McDougall famously repelled a hostile takeover by Goodman Fielder Wattie in 1988 by producing brand valuations that demonstrated that the bid price dramatically undervalued the business.

However, companies can report on their brands elsewhere in the report and accounts – and this is arguably a more productive approach. There is growing demand from investors and senior management for meaningful information on the company's brands, how they are being managed, and with what results, which is why the 'evaluation' that goes into the 'valuation' of brands is such an important task for marketers.

4.4

BUILDING A BRAND

There may well be a gap between a brand's vision and its image, and marketing has to close or eliminate this in order to sustain trust with its stakeholders. The task is made more difficult in the digital world where infinite amounts of information on any brand is available instantly. There are a number of brand models they can choose from to help them in their task.

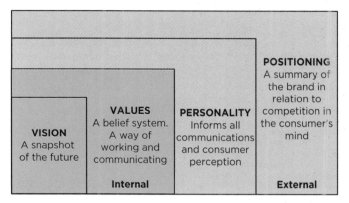

Fig 4.5 The Brand Onion (*Adapted from Interbrand, 2002*)

So-called because of its layers, starting with the vision of what the brand should be, the 'Brand Onion' reveals the heart, or core, of the marketing offer, along with the layers that make it up, including brand values (such as the emotional content), 'personality' and desired position in the marketplace. It includes brand attributes, such as its physical and technical properties, and functional brand benefits.

You determine the information that makes up the layers of a Brand Onion through a brand audit, based on market research.

Personality is agreed to be a highly important aspect of a brand, because research has shown that consumers' perceptions and expectations about brands are not limited to their functional characteristics and advantages. The US social psychologist and marketing professor Jennifer Aaker (1997) developed a framework for measuring brand personality, which she broke down into five core dimensions:

- **Sincerity** – down-to-earth, honest, wholesome, cheerful.
- **Excitement** – daring, spirited, imaginative, up-to-date.
- **Competence** – reliable, intelligent, successful.
- **Sophistication** – upper-class, charming.
- **Ruggedness** – 'outdoorsy', tough.

These five core dimensions all have a number of different traits associated with them. Marketers can decide where they want to position their particular brand, and devise brand strategies accordingly.

Kapferer's Brand Prism (1997), depicted in Fig 4.6, is another model for branding. The model has six facets:

- **Physique** – the basis of the brand. The physique of Volvo would be safety and reliability, for example.
- **Personality** – as in Aaker's personality model, 'what if this brand were a person?'
- **Culture** – symbolises the organisation and the values of its country-of-origin. For example, for SEAT this would be 'auto-emoción, the passionate Spanish heart of the brand.
- **Relationship** – the 'handshake' between the consumer and the organisation.
- **Reflection** – the consumer's perception of what the brand stands for. Coca-Cola is perceived as a young, fun lifestyle brand for example.
- **Self-image** – the customer's own image, projected onto the brand, or vice-versa.

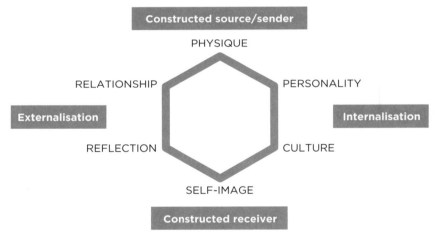

Fig 4.6 The Brand Prism (*adapted from Kapferer, 1997*)

THE BRANDING PENTAGRAM

Branding is optimal when the real brand experience matches the desired brand experience. The Branding Pentagram is a framework for evaluating and elaborating five integral factors that influence branding strategy, and thus help to translate corporate strategy into everyday actions that create the desired brand experience. See Figure 4.7.

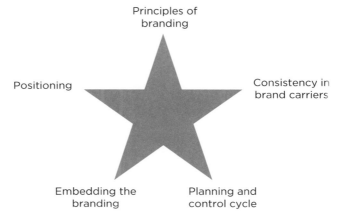

Principles of
branding

Positioning

Consistency in
brand carriers

Embedding the
branding

Planning and
control cycle

Fig 4.7 The Brand Pentagram (*adapted from Baker and Hart*)

1. **Principles of branding**
   - **Brand mission** – which goals do I eventually want to achieve with the brand?
   - **Desired brand perception** – what are the core values of the brand?
   - **Brand architecture** – what are my choices regarding the brand portfolio?

2. **Positioning**
   - **Segmentation** – what segmentation criteria are used?
   - **Target group** – what group(s) is the brand aimed at (client/end user)?
   - **Position** – how does the brand distinguish itself compared to (the critical success factors of) the competitors? This should be measured both in terms of the product offered (the proposal to the clients) and the performance of the organisation (the clients' perception).

3. **Consistency in brand carriers**
   To maximise the effect of the brand, there must be consistency in the way the brand is carried. This can be done by creating consistency in the way the brand is carried by the different products and services of the organisation, and by how the brand is 'carried out' and spoken of by the employees of the organisation or an intermediary. Further consistency can be guarded via the different means the organisation uses to communicate.

4. **Embedding the branding**
   This starts by ensuring consistency. The brand policy needs to align consistently with underlying functions and responsibilities. Responsibilities and authority for branding should be assigned to one of the management team or board members. A person should be appointed who will have direct responsibility for branding. Branding should be embedded by anchoring it in the organisation's culture and the behaviour of its employees.

5. **Planning and control cycle**

   This starts with the formulation of SMART (Specific, Measurable, Achievable, Relevant, Time-bound) targets of brand policy for both the short and the long term. Next, the planning and control cycle can be developed by determining how you are going to measure it. The data to be collected must be capable of being measured using a realistic scale requisite to the task. This measurement then needs to feed back into the planning and control process.

Positioning and repositioning – Brand models such as those described above help the marketer to 'position' his or her brands in a way that differentiates them from the competition by giving them a distinct and valued place in the minds of target consumers. It involves refining the proposition and brand image, as Ries and Trout (1986) explain: "The basic approach of positioning is not to create something new and different, but to manipulate what's already up there in the mind, to re-tie the connections that already exist."

Positioning is a critical marketing task. From a price/value perspective, your product (or service) could be Rolls-Royce or Ford Fiesta, Prada or Primark, Harrods or Lidl. The key thing is to decide on your positioning and communicate it clearly and consistently, because if you don't the market (aided by social media) will do it for you. Fig 4.8 illustrates the required steps.

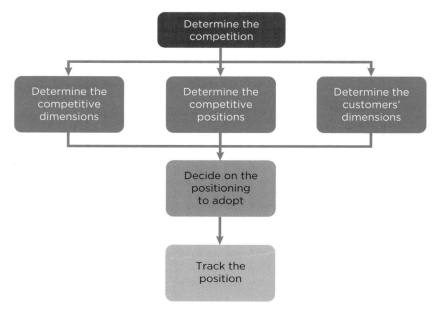

Fig 4.8 How to position a brand

Brand portfolios – Most companies will have a portfolio of brands, so will want to position each of them not just against the competition but also against each other. The brands may well be at a different stages in their product lifecycle and will therefore need very different strategic approaches. Product portfolio models help marketers to visualise the portfolio and classify the brands according to their problems and needs.

The best-known portfolio management tool is the **Boston Consulting Group (BCG) Matrix,** which positions brands according to market growth and relative market share. You calculate relative market share by dividing a brand's share of market (SOM) by the SOM of the largest competitor, and, in the classic version of the matrix, position your brands in four quadrants. The categories are as follows:

- **Star** – A brand in a growing market, with a larger share of market than most. It has good revenues and profits, but usually needs a lot of marketing support.
- **Problem child** – A brand in a growing market but with a small SOM. Such brands have great potential but are also in a risky situation. They are also referred to as **question marks,** because marketers need to work out how the brand might develop.
- **Cash cow** – A brand in a mature market with a large market share. Maintaining its position requires little effort or investment. Such brands generate income, which can be invested in other needy brands.
- **Dog** – A brand also in a stable market but with a small or declining SOM. Unlikely to be profitable, such brands are candidates for phasing out.

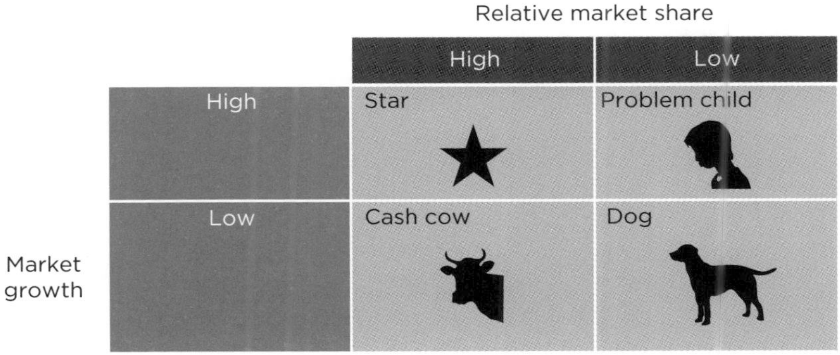

Fig 4.9 The BCG matrix

Carefully positioning and repositioning brands allows you to spot opportunities for developing them. There are three potential strategies to develop successful brands:

- **Brand stretching** – Launching a modified product, or an entirely new product, with the same brand name, into the same or a similar category.
- **Line extension** – Launching a new product closely related to the existing one.
- **Multi-branding** – Having several brands in the same category, as many big organisations often have. Unilever, for example, has many toothpaste brands.

Virgin Group exemplifies brand stretching. Virgin has attracted a lot of criticism from people who believe it has stretched its brand so far – from records and an airline to cola and wedding outfits – that Virgin no longer stands for anything other than its founder Sir Richard Branson.

McDonald's, which is normally very good at sticking to what it knows, has made mistakes. For example, McPizza failed. Consumers just didn't buy it (in any sense).

ACTIVITY 4.2
Calculate the relative market share for each product/brand of your organisation.

QUICK QUIZ – CHECK YOUR KNOWLEDGE
Questions
1. Explain the limitations of the product lifecycle.
2. Which is the correct sequence in NPD?
    a. Idea screening, commercialisation, business analysis.
    b. Idea screening, commercialisation, concept testing.
    c. Idea screening, business analysis, market testing.
3. Name the typical layers of the Brand Onion.
4. What is the Ladder of Loyalty?
5. According to Jennifer Aaker, what is brand personality?
6. In the BCG Matrix, what is a 'star'?

Answers
1. It can be difficult to determine the stage reached, and how long each stage will last; the length of time in any stage is highly variable, so you can't use it for forecasting; brands don't necessarily become obsolete; and the model over-emphasises NPD at the expense of mature products.
2. c.
3. Vision, values, personality, positioning.

4. The relationship with customers is visualised in terms of climbing the rungs an imaginary ladder, with marketing's task being to move potential customers (starting with a prospect) up the ladder through branding and relationship marketing.
5. Aaker breaks down brand personality into five components: sincerity, excitement, competence, sophistication and ruggedness.
6. A brand in a growing market, with a larger SOM than most, but which, despite good revenues and profits, usually needs a lot of marketing support.

FURTHER READING

Fill, C. and Turnbull, S. (2016) *Marketing communications: discovery, creation and conversations*. 7th edition. Harlow, Pearson. ISBN 9781292092614 Chapter 9 pp287–322 and Chapter 12 pp355–382.

References

Aaker, D. A. (1991) *Managing brand equity: capitalizing on the value of the brand name*. US, Jossey Bass.

Aaker, J. (1997) Dimensions of brand personality. *Journal of Marketing Research*, August, pp347–356.

Aaker, D. (2014) *Aaker on branding: 20 principles that drive success*. Morgan James Publishing.

Anon (2013) Shell and Ferrari. *Shell*. http://www.shell.com/global/products-services/on-the-road/oils-lubricants/cars/shell-oils/shell-ferrari.html

Anon (2017) BrandZ™. Kantar Millward Brown. http://www.millwardbrown.com/brandz/brandz

Baker, M and Hart, S. (1999) *Product strategy and management*. Harlow, Pearson.

Brassington, F. and Pettitt, S. (2006) *Principles of marketing*. 4th edition. Harlow, Prentice Hall.

Christopher, M., Payne, A. and Ballantyne, D. (2002) *Relationship marketing: creating stakeholder value*. Abingdon, Routledge.

Kapferer, J-N. (1997) *Strategic brand management*. 2nd edition. London, Kogan Page.

Keller, K.L. (2008) *Strategic brand management: building, measuring, and managing brand equity*. 3rd edition. NJ, Pearson Education.

McDonald, M. and Wilson, H. (2011) *Marketing plans: how to prepare them, how to use them*. 7th edition. Chichester, John Wiley.

Ries, A. and Trout, J. (1986) *Positioning: the battle for your mind*. McGraw-Hill.

You Tube
The new Apple (RED) iPhone 7 is Here! (2017) YouTube video, 21 March, Soldier Knows Best https://www.youtube.com/watch?v=c7G4UlpmvT4

Apple Watch Review: is it pointless (2015) YouTube video, 10 May, Soldier Knows Best https://www.youtube.com/watch?v=BoPHWtoHWqc&t=28s

Shell and Ferrari Circuit TV ad (2012) YouTube video, 31 October, Shell https://www.youtube.com/watch?v=pRPMdY6hg50

5.

MARKETING COMMUNICATIONS: UNDERSTANDING THE COMPONENTS OF THE MIX

OUTLINE

This chapter starts to examine the 'mix' of marketing communications, including the different forms of promotional media, both on- and offline, and their strengths and limitations. We also consider current marketing communications issues, including media developments such as media fragmentation and the impact of the internet. At the end of this chapter you will be able to do the following:

- Compare marketing communications methods.
- Identify and evaluate different forms of media.
- Understand how to apply communications tools in different contexts.
- Understand how to use communications to manage corporate reputation.

GLOSSARY

Marketing communications is concerned with the methods, processes, meanings, perceptions and actions that audiences (consumers and organisations) undertake with regards to the presentation, consideration and actions associated with products, services and brands. (Fill 2016)

Marketing communications comprise: "all the promotional elements of the marketing mix which involve the communications between an organisation and its target audiences on all matters that affect marketing performance." (Pickton and Broderick, 2005).

MARKETING COMMUNICATIONS METHODS

Promotion as part of the 4P marketing mix

The marketing mix is the core of marketing. It is traditionally expressed as either the 4Ps (product, price, place and promotion) or the 7Ps (the 4Ps plus people, process and physical evidence). Marketing communications is the fourth P – the 'promotion' element of the marketing mix – and it encompasses the following:

- Advertising.
- Sales promotion.
- Public relations (PR).
- Personal selling.
- Direct marketing.
- The full range of digital marketing techniques, including social media, pay per click, online display advertising, email marketing etc, all of which are growing strongly.

These key areas of promotional activity make up a business's total marketing communications programme, referred to as the 'promotional mix'. See Fig 5.1.

Fig 5.1 The promotional mix

Elements that don't fit neatly into the above labelling but are increasingly significant include the following.

- **Ambient advertising** – advertising outside the home using non-traditional media, such as beer mats, the backs of supermarket till receipts and panels in toilets. Also called 'proximity media'.
- **Word of mouth (WOM)** – arguably the most powerful medium, amplified by viral marketing, particularly through social media.
- **Product placement** – careful placement of brands in films or TV shows. In 2015 Audi appeared in *Fifty Shades of Grey* and Mercedes-Benz in *Jurassic World*, for example, and Heineken beer and Omega watches in the 2012 James Bond movie *Skyfall*.

Promotional objectives
Communication has four main purposes. Fill (2016) uses the mnemonic **DRIP** to succinctly sum these up:

- **D**ifferentiate.
- **R**emind (Reassure).
- **I**nform.
- **P**ersuade.

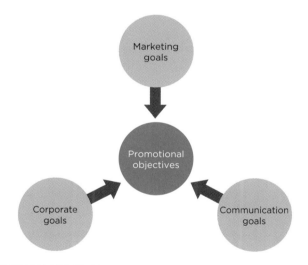

Fig 5.2 Promotional objectives

Most communication will have at least one of these four factors as its main objective, and it can be useful to analyse which factor is most important for your brand when putting a message together.

Fill (2016) also says that the primary role of marketing communications is to engage audiences at an intellectual and emotional level:

"When engagement occurs an individual might be said to have been positively captivated and, as a result, opportunities for further communication activities should increase. Engagement involves attention-getting and awareness but it also encompasses the decoding and processing of information at a conscious or subconscious level, so that meaning can be attributed to a message at the appropriate time."

Choosing the right combination of promotional tools – the right promotional mix – to meet the communications objectives is the key to successful marketing communications.

- **Above-the-line promotion** – Advertising placed in paid-for media, such as print media (newspapers and magazines), radio, TV, cinema and outdoor/transport poster sites. The 'line' refers to the line in an advertising agency's accounts – the figures *above* the line represent the commission it makes from buying media space for clients.
- **Below-the-line promotion** – A blanket term for a range of non-commission-earning marketing communication activities, such as sales promotion and direct marketing – and agencies' fees for these appear *below* the line in their accounts.
- **Through-the-line** – A more recent strategic approach that involves both of the above. Through-the-line communications allow for a consistent integrated strategy across all media, including digital media. These days we are more likely to call this approach 'multi-channel' or 'omni-channel' marketing.
- **Permission marketing** – Implies the need to treat customers with respect, recognising their right to refuse to be bombarded with product and service offerings. But once customers have agreed to being targeted, you can direct tailored and relevant messages at them. This term was popularised by the US digital guru Seth Godin in his book *Permission Marketing* (1999).

The promotional mix
Figure 5.3 gives an indication of the variety of communication tools available to the marketer. As the diagram suggests, the range of communication methods can be seen as targeting three broad groups:

1. Consumer audiences.
2. Audiences in distribution channels.
3. All stakeholder audiences.

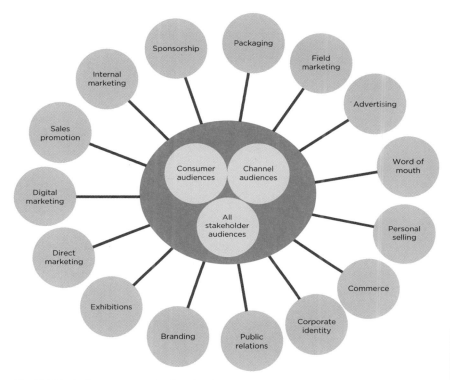

Fig 5.3 Marketing communication tools

Let's look at some of these in more detail.

Advertising

Traditional advertising (in 'paid-for media') has long been the main staple for reaching consumer audiences, as well as members of the other two groups, including 'internal customers' (your colleagues). Advertising is a non-personal form of mass communication.

The American Marketing Association (2017) defines advertising as follows.

"The placement of announcements and persuasive messages in time or space purchased in any of the mass media by business firms, nonprofit organizations, government agencies, and individuals who seek to inform and/ or persuade members of a particular target market or audience about their products, services, organizations, or ideas."

Come to Romania!

In the spring of 2013, *Gandul*, a Romanian newspaper, launched a spoof campaign entitled 'We may not like Britain, but you will love Romania'. Quotas limiting the number of Romanian and Bulgarian immigrants allowed to live and work unrestricted in Britain were to expire in January 2014, and the Romanian campaign was a response to the UK government's reported intention to conduct an anti-immigration campaign in Romania. A government source told *The Guardian* newspaper that the intention of the campaign was to inform prospective immigrants that Britain's streets are not necessarily 'paved with gold'.

In Britain, the government's proposed negative ad campaign (or 'de-marketing' action) was derided, and *The Guardian* invited readers to imagine what such a campaign might look like. Readers' humorous suggestions focused on our poor weather, lack of jobs and unpopular political situation. *Gandul* countered with a humorous campaign designed to attract British people to Romania: the newspaper asked for readers' suggestions via a 'Come to Romania' app.

Here's a sample of readers' suggestions:

- 'Charles bought a house here in 2005. And Harry has never been photographed naked once.'
- 'Our draft beer is less expensive than your bottled water.'
- One of the more tongue-in-cheek suggestions was a poster claiming: 'Half of our women look like Kate. The other half look like her sister'.

Here, we see DRIP used (albeit humorously) to defend a country's reputation. In the past one of Romania's favourite chocolate bars, ROM, launched a campaign entitled 'Romanians are smart', which played on patriotism.

ACTIVITY 5.1

In September 2014, the Scots went to the polls to vote on whether their country should remain part of the United Kingdom. For many, it seems, the antidote to the global misery that followed the 2007/2008 banking crisis in the West is to 'think smaller and think local'. On the other hand, big multinational corporations want to be seen as your friendly 'local shop'. Even charities, like British Heart Foundation, for example, are trying to create more of a local flavour with their fundraising, to counter perceptions of 'big, faceless, corporate' charities. HSBC dropped its 'world's local bank' positioning several years ago, but McDonald's manages the balance well. See http://www.global-strategy.net/how-do-you-balance-global-and-local/.

Discuss this in class or, if you're studying alone, outline your thoughts on 'global versus local' and potential strategies for different product categories.

For more examples of how be 'glocal', follow these links:

https://www.ama.org/publications/MarketingNews/Pages/achieving-glocal-success.aspx

https://www.forbes.com/sites/sylviavorhausersmith/2012/06/22/cultural-homogeneity-is-not-an-automatic-by-product-of-globalization/#5be71f6f5034

http://www.shortpress.com.au/why-your-brand-needs-a-glocal-strategy-and-its-not-just-a-buzzword

https://qz.com/1036380/ikea-catalogue-2017-defining-domestic-bliss-in-different-cultures/

Traditional advertising can be highly effective for many different purposes, usually for a large target audience. For example, it can:

- Promote or create a desired image in the public consciousness.
- Represent a 'call to action'.
- Remind and reassure people.
- Support other promotional tools, including PR, direct marketing and sales.
- Counter negative public opinion.
- Reach a large audience, very quickly.
- Be the least expensive medium, in absolute cost terms.

However, it also has disadvantages:

- **Wastage** – The old adage that "half my advertising is wasted, but I don't know which half" is true of most advertising, but especially TV advertising.
- **Interactivity** – It is usually a one-way street. Unless you use direct response advertising, no feedback is possible. It is a 'message in a bottle'.
- **High investment** – TV advertising can be expensive, not just to buy space but also to produce the commercials.

Wells Fargo tries to make things right

In September 2016 Wells Fargo launched a TV advertising campaign as part of a drive to repair the bank's reputation after a scandal of faked accounts. The ads ran on high-profile US news programmes and talk shows, and while they didn't actually apologise, they assured viewers that they were 'making changes to make things right'.

Employees had set up as many as two million bogus accounts for customers without their permission, targeting the old, students and people who spoke little English. Employees were, in essence, 'gaming' the incentive system the bank had introduced to drive growth. The bank was forced to pay millions of dollars to customers and in fines, its credit rating fell and customers defected to competitors.

The TV ads, which complemented a print and digital campaign, were designed to spread awareness of what the bank was doing to address the problems. They featured historic horse-drawn wagons, beautiful countryside and a reassuring female narrator, in an effort to remind people of the brand's long and illustrious heritage. They also made ads about the making of the ads, including building the coaches and training the horses.

Wells Fargo knows to its cost the truth of the old adage that it takes years of hard work to build a reputation - but that reputation can be lost overnight. It looks likely to have to keep up the marketing momentum for some time to come. In May 2017 CNBC reported that lawyers for the alleged victims of the fake account scandal say that Wells Fargo may have been responsible for more unauthorised accounts than previously thought.

https://www.youtube.com/watch?v=uh3zleQY-QY

Sales promotion

Sales promotion provides 'added-value' to an offering with the aim of accelerating sales and gathering marketing information. Providing 'extra benefit' offers for a limited time period, it is usually seen as a short-term tactical tool – for generating trial, repeat purchase, or both, for example – but it can devalue a brand's image. Integrating sales promotion with direct marketing, however, can be highly effective.

Sales promotion can be used to:

- defend shelf space and add interest in store.
- control demand, especially during 'low season'.
- instil a sense of urgency such as 'buy now!'
- price-discriminate among customer segments.

There are disadvantages:

- It is usually unable to deliver a personalised message credibly, unless the vehicle is direct marketing.
- Credibility is low to medium, and it may actually harm the brand.

Public relations (PR)

PR can be an exceptionally powerful weapon, particularly in business-to-business (B2B) contexts. It seeks to promote goodwill and build mutual understanding across all the various publics. PR encompasses events, lobbying, crisis management, image building and lead generation, all at a lower cost than advertising. The PR department is often responsible for internal marketing too. PR is seen as one of the most credible forms of promotion, which makes it a good tool to manage corporate reputation and crises. It is also a useful tool for reaching specific audiences. Companies use PR to create publicity or 'earned media'. However, PR is subject to many variables and is therefore hard to manage.

The CIM (2014) defines PR as "the function or activity that aims to establish and protect the reputation of a company or brand, and to create mutual understanding between the organisation and the segments of the public with whom it needs to communicate."

PR works with at least ten different audience groups:

- The community.
- Potential employees.
- Employees.
- Suppliers of services and materials.
- Investors.
- Distributors.
- Consumers/customers.
- Opinion leaders.
- Trade unions.
- The media.

The tools of PR include:

- Press releases.
- Press conferences.
- Publications.
- Media relations.

- Events.
- Annual reports.
- Lobbying.
- Internal PR.
- Social media channels.

Personal selling
Personal selling is often associated with face-to-face activities but increasingly this contact may occur via other methods of communication such as teleconference, videoconference etc.. Its advantages include the following:

- It can win high customer attention.
- You can customise the message.
- Interactivity improves understanding.
- It is very persuasive.
- You can use it to develop the relationship.

- You can adapt it to different circumstances.
- It offers a better opportunity to close the sale.

There are also disadvantages:

- It is labour-intensive and involves high costs per contact.
- It is time-consuming, so it can reach only a limited number of customers.
- It requires training and flair.
- It requires careful planning.

Direct marketing (DM)

Direct marketing seeks to build one-to-one relationships. It does this by analysing individual customer information, creating databases, devising a creative strategy and personalising messages that require an individual direct response. DM is a marketing channel without intermediaries and is the fastest-growing form of marketing.

Direct marketing has been enhanced over recent years by **digital marketing**, which is essentially about applying internet technologies to the sale and distribution of products and services, as well as being a medium for communicating with the marketplace. Digital marketing covers all form of digital media and communications, including mobile devices.

Forms of direct marketing include the following:

- Personal selling.
- Direct mail (still the most common form).
- Kiosk marketing – either the 'pop-up' type (like those for roadside assistance services, like the AA in the UK) or quasi-permanent (in shopping centres you see jewellers, nail bars, etc).
- Telemarketing (less popular these days, because intrusive and disliked).
- Email (holding its own but consumers are rightly cautious about unsolicited messages).
- Direct response advertising (press/radio/TV).
- Catalogue marketing – convenient and offers ready access to a huge range of products.
- Company blogs and (to some extent) company reports. Blogs offer fresh, original and inexpensive ways to reach fragmented audiences but, because of their 'personal' nature, are difficult to control.
- Internet/e-commerce (websites) are interactive and immediate. The huge expansion of online shopping over the past decade or more shows no sign of slowing. Social media marketing can also be highly effective, when handled carefully.
- Mobile marketing (including smartphones, SMS text messaging and tablets). Currently enjoying a boom and set to become increasingly significant as it develops further, helped by more ubiquitous 4G

technology and the advent of 5G, which is expected to start rolling out globally in 2020. For more information on location-based mobile marketing, follow this link. http://www.adweek.com/brand-marketing/5-ways-location-based-marketing-will-evolve-2017-175204/. In the UK, marketing via SMS/MMS and so on is subject to the non-broadcast code (the CAP Code). The ASA regulates text messages if they are advertisements.

DM can be used with great effect to:

- personalise offers by using existing customer profiles.
- target prospects who have had previous contact with the company.
- target risk-averse consumers.
- target customers looking for a high level of service.

There are few disadvantages to DM, provided campaigns are well-structured and integrated with other promotional tools such as advertising. Nevertheless, some things can go wrong:

- Faulty, out-of-date or ill-conceived databases.
- Poorly crafted DM goes straight into the 'junk mail' folder.
- With changes in data protection laws due to take effect in May 2018, direct marketing may become a more important channel once more.

Be warned, however: direct marketing is highly regulated. You must always check if customers want to be contacted by fax, phone, post or email, and give them the chance to object. When you collect customer details you must get their permission if you want to send them other offers or promotions, or if you want to share their information with another organisation. You must make it easy for them to opt out. For a list of regulations covering direct marketing go to https://www.gov.uk/marketing-advertising-law/direct-marketing

REAL LIFE 5.5

Kit Kat surely wins

Kit Kat is very similar to the Japanese phrase 'Kitto Katsu', which translates as 'will surely win', and the brand had long been considered a good luck charm for students preparing for their exams. Kit Kat has built on this with special packages that allow friends and family members to write supportive messages and contain a pyramid screen which, when placed on a smartphone, plays a YouTube video from the pop group DISH// Kit Kat got 33,034 tweets in the first month after the promotion was launched and saw sales rise by 150%. Kit Kat has a range of additional flavours in Japan, including strawberry cheesecake, sweet potato and wasabi.

http://www.thedrum.com/news/2016/01/22/kit-kat-turns-packaging-holograms-japanese-boy-band

Sponsorship

Sponsorship entails supporting an event or activity by providing money (or something else of value to the event organiser), usually in return for 'mentions'.

There are three main typed of sponsorship: programme, arts/sports, and educational.

Sponsorship can build corporate image and align public perception with the organisation's true or intended corporate identity.

However, sponsorship can backfire if the event or individual being sponsored falls out of favour, which they can do – and quickly. Cyclist Lance Armstrong lost 11 sponsors, including Nike and Anheuser-Busch InBev, worth an estimated $150m, after allegations of doping covering the time he won seven consecutive Tour de France titles between 1999 and 2005. Footballer Wayne Rooney lost sponsorship by Coke Zero in the wake of a sex scandal. Tennis player Maria Sharapova lost lucrative sponsorship deals with Porsche, Tag Heuer and Avon after she tested positive for drugs. And a drunken scandal cost an Olympic swimmer a high-profile sponsorship with Speedo.

But brands can also be caught out by not doing their homework. Soon after being chosen as the face of Yardley cosmetics, actress Helena Bonham Carter admitted in an interview that she rarely wore makeup and couldn't understand why the brand had chosen her. The deal ended soon after.

ACTIVITY 5.2

Imagine your line manager is rather conservative when it comes to digital marketing and complains of 'the difficulty in assessing the benefits'. You are preparing for a meeting in which you know you will need to push for further digital activity and greater web presence for your organisation. How will you make your case?

5.2

IDENTIFYING AND EVALUATING DIFFERENT FORMS OF MEDIA

The range of promotional media available to marketing has continued to fragment, mostly because of the rise in digital technology, which provides new online options, not least social media. With nearly 42 million adults in the UK using the internet every day (ONS, 2016), more than double the 2006 figure, the digital age has changed the marketing landscape. Consumers now have 'always on' access to diverse digital platforms via wifi hotspots in coffee shops, pubs and restaurants, on trains and in some cases, such as the City of London, whole areas. This trend of free access will accelerate.

Traditional and non-traditional media options include the following:

- **Broadcast media** – TV (eg popular television) and radio.
- **Print media** – Newspapers (eg the *Sunday Times*, *Times of India*) and magazines (eg *The Economist*).
- **Outdoor media** – Billboards (96-, 48- and six-sheet), street furniture such as bus shelters (through Adshel or J. C. Decaux), speciality signage, digital billboards, mobile billboards, building wraps and projection.
- **Ambient media** – Supermarket trolleys, car park receipts, images projected onto buildings, interactive billboards, litter bins and petrol pumps. (There is clearly some crossover with outdoor media.)
- **Transit media** – Underground and metro stations, bus sides, taxis.
- **New media** – Internet websites/banners/pop-ups/online films/ YouTube; Digital TV; DVD; email; smartphone/tablet.
- **In-store** – Point of purchase, packaging, bins, signs, displays, floor art – for example 3D floor posters targeting consumers at key points with striking visual advertising.
- **Cinema** – Longer-duration commercials.
- **Fairs and exhibitions** – For example Grand Designs, Frankfurt Book Fair.
- **TV shows, films and theatre productions for product placement** – Omega watches and Aston Martin sports cars in Bond movies, for example.
- **Stealth marketing** – The trick of stealth marketing is to make it so subtle that the consumer doesn't realise it's a marketing ploy. For some famous examples see this link https://www.delnext.com/blog/ en/2017/05/stealth-marketing-campaigns/.
- **Experiential marketing** – For example, stunts and flashmobs. Flashmobs are groups of people who assemble suddenly in a public place, perform an unusual and apparently pointless act for a brief time, then quickly disperse. They are organised by text, social media or viral emails. For some examples, see the link https://www.delnext. com/blog/en/2017/05/most-famous-flash-mobs/. For a flashmob with a more serious intent see this link – and watch it to the end https://www.fastcompany.com/3017004/this-sex-worker-flash-mob- dance-video-has-an-extra-twist

- **Guerrilla marketing** – Covers all kinds of alternative media, including street art and flyposting. Some of them are illegal, which means brands are taking a risk in getting involved. See some examples here https://www.delnext.com/blog/en/2017/02/15-examples-guerrilla-marketing/

The list goes on, and is limited only by marketers' imaginations in trying to find ever-more inventive ways to get their messages across to their target audiences.

To compare the benefits of different media you need to use **the '4Cs' of media comparison:**

- **Cost** – How much will the campaign cost, in both absolute and relative terms (cost per thousand contacts, or CPM)? What production costs are involved?
- **Credibility** – This all-important factor derives from the channel, the proximity to relevant programme content and the popularity and credibility of the associated programme. The effects are similar with magazines and radio.
- **Communication effectiveness** – Which media can deliver the message in the most effective way. This considers how the target audience can be reached (targeted or mass market) and by which communications method (audio and/or visual).
- **Control** – How much control the advertiser has over the environment their message appears within, both in terms of surrounding content and the noise within that environment that could influence how the message is received.

You can see the relative effectiveness of different promotional tools in terms of their ability to influence purchase behaviour in Fig 5.4 (below and overleaf). While personal selling is obviously not the best way to gain mass public awareness, when it comes to the nitty-gritty of closing a sale it is the most effective, particularly in a business-to-business context where the value of a sale is high and the decision-making process likely to be lengthy and complex and to involve multiple decision-makers.

	Advertising	Sales promotion	Public relations	Personal selling	Direct marketing
Communications					
Ability to deliver a personal message	Low	Low	Low	High	High
Ability to reach a large audience	High	Medium	Medium	Low	Medium
Level of interaction	Low	Low	Low	High	High
Credibility given by target audience	Low	Medium	High	Medium	Medium
Credibility					
Given by the target audience	Low	Medium	High	Medium	Medium

	Advertising	Sales promotion	Public relations	Personal selling	Direct marketing
Costs					
Absolute costs	High	Medium	Low	High	Medium
Costs per contact	Low	Medium	Low	High	High
Wastage	High	Medium	High	Low	Low
Size of investment	High	Medium	Low	High	Medium
Control					
Ability to target particular audiences	Medium	High	Low	Medium	High
Management's ability to adjust the deployment of the tool as circumstances change	Medium	High	Low	Medium	High

Fig 5.4 The 4Cs framework – a summary of the key characteristics of the tools of marketing communications (*Fill, 2013*)

It is hard to imagine buying a new car without the intervention of a sales person at some point. Personal selling and advertising are at opposite ends of the awareness-purchase spectrum (see Fig 5.5), but work well together in areas such as car sales. Advertising creates high awareness and a call-to-action, but the sales person closes the sale.

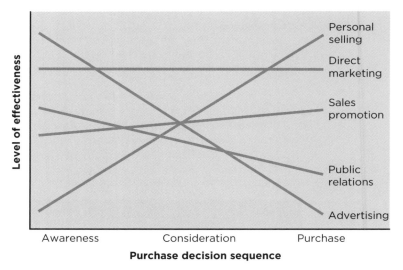

Fig 5.5 The awareness-purchase spectrum (*Fill, 2009*)

Fig 5.6 opposite shows the benefits and drawbacks of the main forms of media.

Media	Characteristics and advantages	Disadvantages
TV	• High reach. • High frequency potential. • Low cost per contact. • Creative opportunities. • High intrusion value. • Segmentation possibilities through programme choice (eg football games for beer commercials). • TV advertising demonstrates competitive strength and supports the sales force.	• Clutter (interference from other ads). • Low recall due to clutter. • Channel surfing during commercials. • Catch-up TV. • Only short amount of copy possible. • High cost per ad (airtime and production). • Repetition essential.
Radio	• Personal and intimate medium. • Campaign reach. • Greater frequency than TV ('opportunity to hear'). • Unlike TV, listeners tend not to change channels when ads are on. • Lower cost per spot than TV. • Lower production cost than TV. • High segmentation potential. • Flexibility in making new ads. • Ability to modify ads quickly and locally. • DJ intimacy. • Out of home listening (in the car or the workplace).	• Short exposure time. • Low attention (listening in shops, or at work, at the garage etc). • Poor ability to reach national audience. • Lacks the prestige of TV. • Very fragmented. • High wastage. • Lacks impact and less able than TV to demonstrate benefits or hold audience attention.
Newspapers	• Coupons and special response ads. • High credibility. • Strong audience interest. • Longer copy. • High flexibility (eg short lead times). • Cumulative volume discounts.	• Clutter (many ads). • Short lifetime span/ ephemeral. • Poor-quality reproduction. • Limited audience.

	• Local ads in regional papers. • Very targeted.	
Magazines	• Specific segmentation, by definition (eg magazines for brides). • High paper/colour quality. • Longer life (may be kept for long periods). • Direct response techniques (coupons). • Read during leisure time. • Longer attention to ads ('dwell time'). • Complicated messages are possible. • Diverse formats, supplements, 'advertorials'.	• Long lead times. • Less flexibility. • High cost. • Clutter. • Declining readership. • Some magazines have low content and are mostly advertising.
Outdoor	• Relatively inexpensive. • Many repeat exposures for one appearance. • Sometimes spectacular.	• 'Brief encounters' (often seen from the car only). • Story told by a picture: no copy.
Cinema	• High technological impact. • Humour and high drama. • Good identifiable segment with disposable income.	• High cost. • Hard to measure results.
Digital	• Even the smallest companies can (and arguably should) have their own website. • Once a professionally produced website exists, both digital and offline channels can be used to drive traffic to the site. • Ecommerce is a route to market every traditional retailer should at least consider. • Viral marketing and 'word of mouse'. • The ubiquity of smartphones has led to a rise in mobile advertising	

Fig 5.6 A comparison of principal advertising media

Now let's expand on the table.

Broadcast media: TV – TV is a comparatively expensive advertising medium – a 30-second spot at prime-time viewing costs in the order of £100,000, while production costs could add a further £100,000 to £500,000. The most expensive commercial ever made, for Chanel No 5 in 2004, cost £18m, featured actress Nicole Kidman, costumes by Karl Lagerfeld, and was directed by renowned film director Baz Luhrmann. In absolute terms the cost is high, but considering a typical 'soap' audience on one TV channel is around seven million viewers, or one-third share (that is, one-third of the people watching TV at that time), the cost per thousand (CPM) is low. A TV commercial (TVC), with its possibility of sound, music, colour and movement, has the edge over all other media in terms of communicating an effective message. On the negative side, you need to run the commercial at least ten times (opportunities to see, or OTS) for it to be effective.

Broadcast media: radio – Although radio is ubiquitous, most people seem able to 'tune out' of advertising messages easily. Radio is a more intimate medium than TV and popular radio presenters feel almost like friends. Increasingly, radio DJs are encouraging audiences to get involved and interact through social media such as Facebook and Twitter.

Print media: newspapers – Newspapers have been gradually losing ground to other media since the 1980s, but on the basis that if you can't beat them you have to join them, they are metamorphosing into digital media. *The Guardian*, for example, is proud to offer web, print, tablet and mobile versions (in that order). See, for example, the 2012 'Three Little Pigs' TVC by BBH for *The Guardian*: http://www.youtube.com/watch?v=vDGrfhJH1P4&feature=kp.

The biggest challenge newspaper publishers face is how to monetise their content (make profit out of it) in a world where people can get 'the news' for free. Many are turning to other forms of revenue, such as ecommerce and selling online display advertising, as well as setting up 'pay walls' to charge readers for access.

Print media: magazines – Like newspapers, magazines can be read anywhere, are often passed from one person to another and frequently end up in doctors' waiting rooms to be read by many. This illustrates the difference between readership (the number of people who read each issue) and circulation (the number of copies sold).

Outdoor – Outdoor advertising is very popular for certain categories, such as cars, travel agents and airlines, which all make very good use of the medium. Interactive billboards, although expensive, make the message even more compelling.

Cinema – It is in the cinema that great film production values can be fully exploited to bring out humour, drama and develop themes. Original versions of commercials aired on TV, such as the one for Chanel No 5, mentioned above, have considerable impact in the cinema.

The internet as an advertising medium – Internet marketing is about applying the internet and related digital facilities to help determine and satisfy marketing objectives. Ecommerce can now involve transactions of every kind and websites can host online advertising (of both their own and others' products and services), with links and the use of affiliate marketing (sometimes called performance marketing).

CIM (2014) describes affiliate marketing as: "A form of marketing or advertising used on the internet. Companies that sell products or services online link to relevant sites. The advertising on the other or 'affiliate' sites is paid for according to results."

An example is Amazon, which pays affiliates (publishers) for each customer introduced via a click-through to Amazon's site. Commission is generally payable only when the merchant (Amazon in this case) actually makes a sale to the end-customer.

5.3

COMMUNICATIONS TOOLS IN DIFFERENT CONTEXTS

The way in which an organisation can communicate will often depend on a number of different factors:

- **Size of market** – Large markets tend to be more competitive and therefore require more communication than a niche market where a more personal relationship is needed.
- **Size of organisation** – In terms of resources available to support communications especially budget.
- **Target audience** – Mass market or closely targeted – are media available to communicate to all?
- **Complexity of Purchase** – More communication may be needed to take the consumer through a complex purchase such as a car. A routine purchase such as a chocolate bar is relatively easy to communicate.
- **Role of Intermediaries** – A channel to market that includes a number of intermediaries will require trade or channel communications to ensure that the end consumer receives a consistent message and experience.

Organisational contexts include the following:

- **Business to consumer (B2C)** – Involves selling goods and services to final consumers.
- **Business to business (B2B)** – Involves selling goods and services, providing information online/offline to businesses and building customer relationships.
- **Not for profit (NFP)** – Charity fundraising for good causes.
- **Government/public sector** – Primarily information campaigns. See Real Life example below.
- **Consumer to business (C2B)** – Involves consumers communicating with companies to send suggestions and questions via company websites.
- **Government to business (G2B), Government to consumer (G2C), and Government to government (G2G).**
- **Consumer to consumer (C2C)** – Communication occurs mostly online between interested parties about a wide range of products and subjects. It can take the form of blogs or other consumer-generated content (CGC) or user-generated content (UGC).

REAL LIFE 5.6

Public information message

BT found a clever way to make people aware of the importance of protecting their personal information online. The film, 'Data to Go', shows what happened when people were asked to 'like' a coffee shop's Facebook pages in exchange for a free coffee and croissant.

While customers waited, a team of researchers outside searched public websites to find as much personal information on them as they could withing three minutes it took to prepare the drink. They radioed the information to the barista, who wrote it on cups and handed it to the unsuspecting customers. Hidden cameras captured customers' baffled reactions and the film ends with the line 'Don't make it easy for fraudsters. Set your privacy settings'.

http://home.bt.com/lifestyle/money/money-tips/coffee-shop-customers-shocked-by-like-stunt-in-cifas-data-to-go-video-11364071638280

Now let's look at some of the different organisational contexts in more detail.

Business to consumer – In FMCG markets, the main elements of the marketing communications mix are as follows:

- **Advertising** – To inspire, enthuse, build awareness, DRIP and, increasingly, drive traffic to the website.
- **Sponsorship** – Providing brands associate themselves with highly appropriate products, sponsorship can be very powerful.
- **Corporate identity** – To emphasise differentiation and competitive edge.
- **Public relations** – For FMCG, this usually means media relations.
- **Product placement** – This can be a very valuable tool, witness the James Bond movies, as mentioned above.
- **Trade promotions** – To strengthen 'sell-in' and make certain the product is stocked and well-displayed.
- **Packaging** – Apart from the convenience factor, this identifies and promotes the brand at the point of sale.
- **Point of purchase/merchandising** – All printed material, video and personal promotion 'in-store'.
- **Direct mail** – Competitions and money-off coupons.
- **Digital** – Websites provide brand knowledge and background that advertising can't, while social media are a two-way street for providing information and getting feedback on brands.
- **Voucher codes/e-coupons** – These entitle consumers to a discount when eating at certain restaurants, like Pizza Express, for example.

Customers in consumer markets typically follow a decision-making process similar to the one in Fig 5.7 opposite.

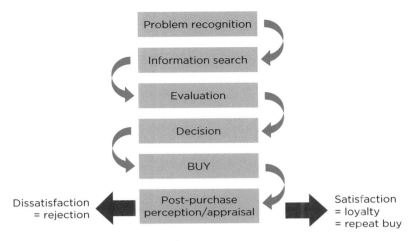

Fig 5.7 The consumer decision-making process

Business to business – With B2B communication, sources of information and the decision-making process itself are different. See Fig 5.8 below.

Fig 5.8 The business decision-making process

Organisations will require much more time to develop the specifications for their particular needs and the search process can be very prolonged. Typically, the professional purchaser will not be the end user and many others are involved in the decision-making unit (DMU).

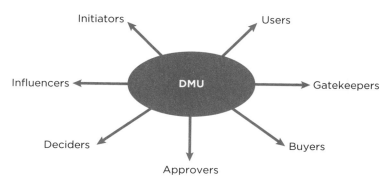

Fig 5.9 The business decision-making unit

REAL LIFE 5.7

We know the future
A new campaign from Intel attempts to allay the fears of future-looking business leaders by personalising 'the future' as a young man who feels insecure and uncool because he frightens people off. The ads reflect a switch in marketing focus for Intel, which has traditionally targeted IT decision-makers. The new campaign targets business managers, who, according to Intel's research, feel anxious that their businesses will be outpaced by emerging technologies. The ads, supported by the endline 'We know the future because we're building it', use a fun, human approach to position Intel as the partner that can build their confidence and raise their excitement about the opportunities the future affords them.

See the ads at

http://creativity-online.com/work/intel-the-future/51540

https://www.skeletonproductions.com/insights/best-b2b-videos

- **Trade advertising** – within sector specific media to inspire, enthuse, build awareness, DRIP and, increasingly, drive traffic to the website.
- **Personal selling** – to focus on the specific customer needs and negotiate how to best meet them through one-to-one relationships.
- **Sponsorship** – in a B2B context, sponsorship of events relevant to the customer can demonstrate a powerful commitment to the relationship.

- **Corporate identity** – to emphasise differentiation and competitive edge.
- **Public relations** – in B2B this creates a positive image for the selling organisation.
- **Trade promotions** – to strengthen 'sell-in' and ensure the product is stocked and well-displayed.
- **Packaging** – this can be adapted to meet different customer needs.
- **Point of purchase/merchandising** – all printed material, video and personal promotion 'in-store'.
- **Direct mail** – to communicate new products or discount proposition.
- **Digital** – websites provide brand knowledge and background that will inform the buyer.

Trade channels and supply chains – Suppliers and other distribution channel members must be 'on the same page' in order to deliver a consistent message in terms of positioning and brand identity to the end user. This is as true in B2B as in B2C markets.

Intranets and extranets (which extend the capacity of an intranet to the supply chain) help marketers to manage channel relationships. They can personalise content by means of 'cookies', which identify users. However, since May 2011, the EU ePrivacy directive requires websites that deposit cookies on people's computers to ask for permission to do so. But the law is still rather unclear, with the UK's Information Commissioner's Office (ICO) adopting a more relaxed approach than some other parts of Europe. On the 10th January 2017 the EU proposed changing the law on cookies. The Regulation of Privacy and Electronic Communications measures would dispense with individual websites' consent pop-ups, pushing the requirement onto web browsers. Watch this space....

Suppliers and, in particular, channels of distribution, merit their own special promotional tools, often referred to under the umbrella term **trade marketing**. In this special case of B2B marketing, possible promotional tools include the following:

- Discounts for trade activities (ie bulk buying).
- Premiums.
- Free merchandise.
- Allowances.
- Dealer listing.
- Dealer loading.
- Sales contests.
- Co-operative advertising.
- Special point-of-sale material.
- House magazines.

Small and medium-sized businesses (SMEs) – Mass market media are typically too expensive for SMEs, yet their target audience, particularly given the marketing reach afforded by the internet, may be global as well as local. Their focus will therefore be on trade advertising, personal selling, PR, direct mail and digital.

Not for profit – While the primary goal of not-for-profit organisations is, as the name suggests, not economic, they may undertake profit-making activities in pursuit of their goal. What's more, because the not-for-profit market is increasingly competitive, such organisations need to deploy the same range of marketing communications activities as FMCG businesses, in order to raise funds. However, they will adapt the message for the donor market, and will emphasise the fact that they will use the money they raise efficiently and effectively.

International and global markets – Companies use digital media and communications tools to adapt their messages to international audiences. They are likely to have country-specific web pages. On a wider scale organisations often employ global advertising agencies to ensure the message is communicated and delivered in a consistent way, albeit tailored to local markets. However, this may not guarantee cultural sensitivity, as German carmaker Audi found recently when an advert in China portraying women as being like second-hand cars sparked outrage in the country. During a wedding ceremony the groom's mother starts to examine the bride, checking her teeth, ears and so on. The advert cuts away to an image of an Audi car with the voiceover "An important decision must be made carefully", before encouraging viewers to visit Audi's second hand car sales website.

In a furious backlash on the internet in China, Audi was criticised for stereotyping the Chinese family as being dominated by an overbearing mother-in-law who rules over the submissive daughter-in-law. However, it seems that the company's marketing in China (and therefore the ad) was the responsibility of its local joint venture partner.

REAL LIFE 5.8

Coca-Cola banned for decades in Portugal
The Portuguese literary giant Fernando Pessoa penned an advertising slogan for Coca-Cola in 1928 that led to the soft drink being banned in the country for 49 years. Already sceptical about its properties, the Lisbon director of health, Dr Ricardo Jorge, banned Coca-Cola and ordered all stocks to be confiscated and thrown into the sea after he learnt of the new slogan: 'Primeiro estranha-se, depois entranha-se!', which translates as 'First you find it strange, then you get it down you!' The slogan seemed to refer to the drink's original supposed association with coca leaves, and Dr Jorge inferred that the inoffensive drink was addictive. Coca-

Cola only managed to overturn the ban and relaunch the brand in Portugal in 1977.

This case is a salutary reminder of the power of slogans, and how easily a name can be misinterpreted. The word 'slogan' derives from an old Scottish word to describe a battle cry – each clan had its own.

Communications tools across contexts

Digital communication – is arguably the most significant development in marketing *ever*. It has created entirely new business opportunities (including ecommerce) and it can be a powerful part of the integrated communications mix, whatever the organisational context and whether you are marketing products or services. There are a number of key issues to consider in digital communications:

- Websites must be truly interactive, with great navigation. They should not just be a list of all the products available, like an online brochure.
- A well-developed website (see Ikea's, for example) creates value for customers because it can be constantly updated – even with 'instant' promotions – and may provide robotic chat or live online chat with someone in the call centre.
- Exploit the endless possibilities to provide an entertaining experience. See, for example, Magnum Treasure Hunt.
- Use search engine optimisation (SEO) to drive traffic to websites.
- Customers can advocate or condemn products and services at will. Driving positive word of mouth (or word of mouse) is a marketing communications imperative.
- Personalisation or mass customisation of products (eg Dell Computers) allows customers to be involved in designing their product, which is likely to increase their satisfaction with it.

QUICK QUIZ – CHECK YOUR KNOWLEDGE

Questions

1. What are the reasons for wastage in the use of TV advertising ?
2. How can Sales promotion be used within a B2B context?
3. Compare how differently personal selling is used in B2B markets and B2C.
4. How can the efficiency of different media be measured?

Answers

1. Time shift viewing through the use of recording devices often allow a viewer to fast forward through commercial breaks. Viewers also take the advantage of a commercial break to do other things – getting a drink, make a call, flick through channels to see what else is on, etc. The growth of 'second' or 'multi-screening' means viewers pay less and less attention to advertising in a commercial breaks.
2. Discounts for bulk purchasing. Additional products/ or services can be provided – for example, free printers with laptop purchases or the additional of a maintenance contract.
Services can be improved – for example, faster delivery times, 24 hour call outs.
Corporate gifts used to be popular, but the practice has declined due to a growing focus on ethical and transparent business. However, corporate entertaining – particularly around sports events – remains popular.
3. In B2B – the salesperson maybe the only form of marketing communication that the buying organisation is aware of. The role of the salesperson is therefore vital in providing information about the product/service and demonstrating that it meets customer expectations. Dealing with objections, minimising risk and negotiating price and delivery are all part of the salespersons remit.
By contrast, the sales person in a B2C context is often responsible only for the transaction and answering some fairly routine questions.
4. Cost per thousand (CPM) is the cost of reaching one thousand of your target audience and can be used to compare relative cost across different media for that target group.

FURTHER READING

Fill, C. and Turnbull, S. (2016) *Marketing communications: discovery, creation and conversations.* 7th edition. Harlow, Pearson. ISBN 9781292092614 Chapters 11–20 pp353–688.

References

Anon (n.d.) Marketing and advertising: the law. www.gov.uk. https://www.gov.uk/marketing-advertising-law/direct-marketing

Anon (n.d.) Coffee shop customers shocked by 'Like' stunt in Cifas Data To Go video. BT.com. http://home.bt.com/lifestyle/money/money-tips/coffee-shop-customers-shocked-by-like-stunt-in-cifas-data-to-go-video-11364071638280

Czinkota, M.R. and Ronkainen, I.A. (n.d.) Achieving 'Glocal' success. https://www.ama.org/publications/MarketingNews/Pages/achieving-glocal-success.aspx

Cockerham, L. (2016) 9 of the best B2B videos ever to inspire your video marketing. 8 August, Skeleton. https://www.skeletonproductions.com/insights/best-b2b-videos

Diaz, A-C. (2017) The future is so not uncool in Intel's B2B campaign. 18 April, Creativity-online. http://creativity-online.com/work/intel-the-future/51540

Fill, C. (2009) *Marketing communications: Interactivity, communities and content.* Fifth edition. Harlow, Financial Times/Prentice Hall.

Fill, C. (2013) *Marketing communications: brands, experiences and participation.* 6th edition. Harlow, Pearson.

Godin, S (1999) *Permission marketing: Turning strangers into friends and friends into customers.* London, Simon & Schuster.

Lynch, R. (n.d.) How to you balance global and local? http://www.global-strategy.net/how-do-you-balance-global-and-local/

Leigh, R. (2016) Passengers given flight discount each time a baby cried on JetBlue Mother's Day stunt. 3rd May. PRexamples http://prexamples.com/2016/05/passengers-given-flight-discount-each-time-a-baby-cried-in-jetblue-mothers-day-stunt/

Leigh, R. (2017) The entire country of Sweden is now listed on Airbnb. 24 May, PRexamples. http://prexamples.com/2017/05/the-entire-country-of-sweden-is-now-listed-on-airbnb/

McEleny, C. (2016) Kit Kat turns packaging into holograms of Japanese boy band. 22 January, The Drum. http://www.thedrum.com/news/2016/01/22/kit-kat-turns-packaging-holograms-japanese-boy-band

ONS (2016) Internet access – households and individuals. ONS https://www.ons.gov.uk/peoplepopulationandcommunity/householdcharacteristics/homeinternetandsocialmediausage/bulletins/internetaccesshouseholdsandindividuals/2016

Pickton, D. W. and Broderick, A. J. (2005) *Integrated marketing communications*. Second edition. Harlow, Financial Times/Prentice Hall.

Quito, A. (2017) How the IKEA catalogue cracked what "domestic bliss" means in different cultures. 25 July, Quartz Media. https://qz.com/1036380/ikea-catalogue-2017-defining-domestic-bliss-in-different-cultures/

Reid, R. D. and Bojanic, D. C. (2010) *Hospitality marketing management*. Fifth edition. Hoboken, John Wiley & Sons, Inc. p400. [AMA definition]

Vorhauser-Smith, S. (2012) Going 'Glocal': how smart brands adapt to foreign markets. 22 July, Forbes. https://www.forbes.com/sites/sylviavorhausersmith/2012/06/22/cultural-homogeneity-is-not-an-automatic-by-product-of-globalization/#5be71f6f5034

Williams, A. (n.d.) Why your brand needs a 'glocal' strategy (and it's not just a buzzword). Shortpress. http://www.shortpress.com.au/why-your-brand-needs-a-glocal-strategy-and-its-not-just-a-buzzword

YouTube
Cannes Lions award-winning "Three Little Pigs" (2012) YouTube, added by *The Guardian*: http://www.youtube.com/watch?v=vDGrfhJH1P4&feature=kp

Wells Fargo commitment campaign (2016) YouTube video, 15 November, Wells Fargo. https://www.youtube.com/watch?v=uh3zleQY-QY

Examples of different forms of media
https://www.delnext.com/blog/en/2017/05/stealth-marketing-campaigns/

https://www.fastcompany.com/3017004/this-sex-worker-flash-mob-dance-video-has-an-extra-twist

https://www.delnext.com/blog/en/2017/05/most-famous-flash-mobs/

https://www.delnext.com/blog/en/2017/02/15-examples-guerrilla-marketing/

6.

DEVELOPING INTEGRATED MARKETING COMMUNICATIONS

OUTLINE

In this chapter we start to look at marketing communications from an integrated standpoint. At the end of this chapter you will be able to do the following:

- Identify appropriate SMART communications objectives.
- Recommend integrated marketing communications (IMC) plans.
- Identify links between internal and external communications.
- Measure the effectiveness of IMC.

However, much of what is covered in this chapter is also covered within the preceding chapters and is brought together here.

INTRODUCTION

It may be useful at this point to recap on the definitions of integrated marketing communications that we included in the glossary to Chapter 1.

The Journal of Integrated Marketing Communication (2014) describes integrated marketing communications as: "a strategic marketing process specifically designed to ensure that all messaging and communications strategies are unified across all channels and are centred around the customer. The IMC process emphasises identifying and assessing customer prospects, tailoring messaging to customers and prospects that are both serviceable and profitable, and evaluating the success of these efforts to minimise waste and transform marketing from an expense into a profit-centre."

Fill (2016) points out that all the tools of marketing communications can reinforce and complement each other to create a more powerful, persuasive and consistent 'message', whether that message is to try a product, keep buying it, or trust the organisation that produced it. For example, he believes that a closer alliance between advertising and PR would be particularly beneficial.

Integrated marketing communications therefore also needs to be integrated with the overall organisational strategy, and involve communications between everyone in the organisation. Historically not only have organisations operated in functional silos – finance, marketing, HR etc – but also, different elements of marketing – advertising, PR, sales promotion and so on – have also been handled by different groups within the organisation. The result is conflict, confusion and duplication.

Cross-functional working is increasingly common, which in itself fosters a more integrated approach, and internal marketing can act as the 'glue' by getting everyone focused on the same organisational objectives – which, in most cases, will be to drive profits through increased sales to loyal customers (or the equivalent in non-profit-making organisations).

It is the responsibility of senior management (the CMO, COO, CEO and CFO) to ensure, with the help of everyone in the organisation as well as external stakeholders (including agency partners), that the activities of the brand or brands, both corporate and product or service, through various online and offline marketing channels, are smoothly integrated and strategically and creatively consistent in order to maximise the return on the total marketing investment. This was a difficult challenge even before the number of channels proliferated as a result of digital technologies. But today the challenge is even greater, which is why, although some organisations do integration better than others, few do it outstandingly well.

Clearly, different media work in different ways: you can't just replicate the look and feel of TV advertising in a website, for example. Coca-Cola exemplifies an integrated communications approach, striving for 'one sound, one sight, one sell' to cut through the cluttered and noisy promotional landscape.

Setting SMART objectives

When setting objectives for an integrated communications campaign, marketers must ensure that they are 'SMART' – that is, specific, achievable, relevant, targeted and timed. This not only helps to clarify thinking, it also makes it easier to evaluate the results.

Specific – What variable is the campaign intended to influence? For example, awareness, perception or attitudes?

Measurable – For example, a percentage level of desired prompted awareness in the target market.

Achievable – If they aren't achievable, people won't be motivated.

Realistic – The actions must be grounded in reality and be relevant.

Targeted and timed – What's the target audience, how precisely is it defined, and over what period are the results to be generated?

Marketers should set multiple SMART objectives: the primary one is likely to be business-orientated, preferably profit, but behavioural and communications objectives need to be set too.

ACTIVITY 6.1

Coca-Cola has always embraced the brand value of 'happiness' and the concept of sharing good times with people we like. A recent and controversial example of this in practice was the 'Small World machines' campaign.

https://www.youtube.com/watch?v=ts_4vOUDImE

Was Coca-Cola trying to bring the people of Indian and Pakistan together for the genuine benefit of both countries? Or just trying to sell more soft drinks? Is it possible and acceptable to do both?

ACTIVITY 6.2

At the heart of the organisation is its *raison d'être* (why it is in business), often expressed through its mission statement. Can you relate your own organisation's mission statement to its expressed objectives? Can you distinguish (generally) between objectives, aims, goals, targets and so on? Are these terms synonymous, or does each have a distinct meaning?

Corporate reputation – One of the most important roles of integrated marketing communications is to build and maintain corporate reputation, and to manage threats to it. The internet, which allows bad news to spread around the world instantaneously, makes this element of communications more critical than ever. Corporate reputation depends on strong brands and strong organisational values and management practices, but stakeholders are quick to point out gaps between what the company purports to be, or sincerely believes it is, and what it actually is. If the gap is large, hard-earned trust can evaporate overnight. One of the more dramatic examples of recent years is the BP Deepwater Horizon oil-spill disaster in 2010, which left the company's sustainability credentials (encapsulated in its 'Beyond Petroleum' positioning) in tatters.

Fombrun (1996) defines corporate reputation as: "the overall estimation in which a company is held by its constituents."

Marketing communication plans need to take full account of an organisation's current and desired reputation, with communications designed to address any gaps or potential gaps between the two. **Gap analysis** can be helpful here. Gaps may take a number of different forms:

* **Personality/identity gap** – A mismatch between what the organisation actually is and how it wishes to be seen.
* **Identity/corporate communication gap** – A mismatch between how the organisation wishes to be seen and what it says about itself.
* **Corporate communication/image gap** – A mismatch between what the organisation says about itself and what audiences perceive.
* **Corporate communication/personality gap** – A mismatch between what the organisation says about itself and what it is actually like.

Companies need to communicate internally and externally to address such mismatches, as Van Riel and Fombrun (2007) point out: "At a time when companies perform in the harsh glare of the media, how long can a company say one thing, while being another, without losing credibility and reputation internally and externally?"

Balmer's 'AC^{2}ID Test' model (2001) examines the different dimensions of corporate identity.

1. **Actual identity** – The reality of the organisation.
2. **Communicated identity (controllable)** – The identity projected by programmes such as advertising, PR, sponsorship and branding.
3. **Communicated identity (uncontrollable)** – News coverage, word of mouth, lobbyists and (increasingly) internet communities.
4. **Conceived identity** – Perceptions of the organisation held by relevant stakeholders, and therefore reflecting 'corporate image' and/or 'corporate reputation'.
5. **Ideal identity** – The optimum positioning for the organisation.
6. **Desired identity** – Top management's vision of how the organisation is to be seen (which may not be the same as a rational assessment of ideal identity).

Clearly, while there can be gaps and mismatches in an organisation's reputation, a controlled communications approach can successfully address them.

COMMUNICATIONS PLANNING

Today's consumers are different in two key ways from those of even ten years ago, as a result of two major changes.

The financial collapse of 2008 and subsequent recession in Europe changed the behaviour of consumers - not least because of the government's 'austerity agenda', which, apart from anything else, has capped pay rises to the UK's millions of public sector workers. 'Value propositions' became very appealing - witness the success of 'discounters' such as Aldi and Lidl. While spending has returned to more normal levels, there is anxiety over the impact that Britain's exit from the European Union will have on prices. Marketers are therefore having to work harder than they did ten years ago to give people reasons to buy.

The internet and growing digitisation has revolutionsed the way we all live and work. Traditional businesses have had to completely rethink the way they market and sell their products and services, not least to compete with the raft of new businesses that have sprung up on the back of the technology revolution. Creating messages that consumers notice and act on is increasingly difficult in today's fast moving, multi-channel world.

The net effect of these two big shifts is that marketing communications have to work harder than ever to change consumer awareness, attitudes and behaviour.

REAL LIFE 6.1

The Government and Public Sector Practice of global communications company WPP has produced a practical guide on how to use integrated communication campaigns to help change citizens' behaviour. The guide includes a case study on how an integrated communication campaign by the New South Wales Fire Service in Australia helped people prepare better for bush fires and overcome the 'it won't happen to me' syndrome. Another case study looks at how the Kenya Revenue Authority used an integrated communication campaign to encourage more people to make their tax payments online.

https://www.wpp.com/govtpractice/reports/integrated-comms-behaviour-change/

(Registration required)

6.2

Context analysis

Just as you do a marketing audit when putting together a marketing strategy and plans, so you should look at the context in which marketing communication occurs. They are both vital steps in the planning process. Context analysis attempts to identify the key market and communication drivers that are influencing the organisation and will affect its ability to achieve its objectives. The main elements of the context analysis are as follows:

- **The customer context** – Segment characteristics, customer perception and attitudes towards the organisation, levels of involvement and perceived risk, the characteristics of the decision-making process, media usage.
- **The business context** – Corporate and marketing strategy, brand and competitive organisation analysis.
- **The internal context** – Corporate identity, organisational culture, resources, strengths and weaknesses.
- **The external context** – The nature and power of key stakeholders, PEST (or PESTELE) considerations, opportunities and threats, the degree of competitive rivalry.

The context analysis will inform communications objectives, positioning and strategy which leads to the selection of the creative message and the appropriate media to convey that message. (See also Chapters 3 and 5).

Business, marketing and communications objectives

Marketing communications objectives cascade down from marketing objectives, which in turn cascade down from organisational objectives, which in turn stem from the organisation's mission statement.

McKay (1972) says there are three basic marketing objectives:

1. Enlarge the market.
2. Increase share of the existing market.
3. Improve profitability with existing market share.

As we have seen earlier in this study guide, marketing communications objectives include the following:

- Changing customer perceptions.
- Creating/building awareness among the target group.
- Positioning (or re-positioning) a product/service.
- Influencing the target audience.
- Improving customer retention.
- Improving customer satisfaction.

- Supporting the launch of a new product.
- Generating sales (volumes and/or revenues).

Setting the right objectives is vital, as they will determine the communication strategy as well as the campaign mix of media and the message content.

Marketing communication strategy

Whether the factors driving the communications strategy are corporate or brand led, the main goal of integrated marketing communications is to influence customer buying behaviour. Using a framework to analyse the entire process helps marketers to see the big picture and enables them to make decisions that link each part of the communications plan together.

In Chapter 3 we looked at Pickton and Broderick's RABOSTIC approach to planning. An alternative framework is Fill's Marketing Communications Planning Framework (MCPF). Neither is 'right' or 'wrong'; marketers can choose the one they find most helpful. Marketing theory often offers such different interpretations.

Fig 6.1 The Marketing Communications Planning Framework (MCPF). (*Fill, 2016*)

According to Fill (2016) marketing communication plans should consist of the following elements:

- Context analysis.
- Communication objectives.
- Marketing communication strategy.
- Co-ordinated communications mix (tools, media and content).
- Resources (human and financial).
- Scheduling and implementation.

- Evaluation and control.
- Feedback.

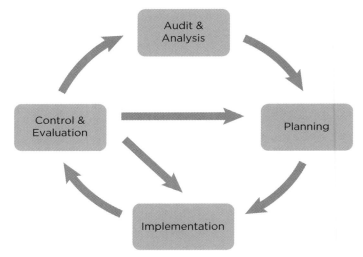

Fig 6.2 APIC model

APIC, which stands for **Analysis, Planning, Implementation and Control**, is another marketing planning model.

Step 1: Audit and analysis. In a new business, this process leads quickly to the initial business planning and objective/goal setting. An existing business would typically do this level of analysis and planning as the result of a major event like recession, significant competitor activity or major technology change. Most companies will review their audit, analysis and planning stages on an annual basis.

Step 2: Planning. This stage creates the marketing plan, based on the results of the audit and analysis; and marketing objectives, strategy and overall tactical plans. Everything will be aligned with the overall corporate mission, strategies and objectives.

Step 3: Implementation. This consists of the marketing and promotional mix, and includes communicating and delivering activities derived from media plans.

Step 4: Control and evaluation. Here you assess how well you've performed, using metrics including how well you meet customer expectations, strengths/weaknesses, and how well you can meet/exceed customer expectations in the future given know opportunities and threats.

At the end of the process, the information produced in the control and evaluation stage feeds back into the overall planning and implementation cycle, which you will continue to adjust and tweak with every cycle.

Multi-channel co-ordinated communications – Organisations can no longer reach their public through a single channel. Markets and audiences are fragmenting as fast as media. TV channels are proliferating and the internet has provided many possibilities for new business models and for new forms of marketing communication. As we saw in Chapter 5, consumers are spending more and more time on internet-related activities. Websites are becoming increasingly interactive, and concepts such as chatbots (computer programmes designed to simulate intelligent conversation) and voice and face recognition software are becoming a reality.

Online advertising available to marketers now goes beyond the classic banners and pop-ups to include 'rich media' and interactive video. (MediaMind, 2013). Moreover online activity has to translate across all devices, from desktop PC to laptop to tablet to smartphone, and users' experience must be consistent and excellent whatever device they use. The latest approach to this challenge is 'responsive design', whereby the website establishes by means of a 'media query' what category of device the user is on, and serves up a tailored version (of a website for example) that is optimised for that particular screen size and web browser. Today, brands that don't provide mobile-optimised user interfaces risk being rejected by customers.

Mobile marketing – Many people are predicting that mobile devices will soon be the primary medium for marketing and advertising. As the technology evolves, mobile is becoming ever more convenient for customers, who are increasingly using their smartphones for everything they used to do on a computer. However, m-commerce – that is, direct sales via a mobile device – is different from mobile branding communications – which are 'consumed' via a mobile device. Most mobile efforts are currently about branding, but it won't be long before they extend to consultation and purchasing decisions too.

The key for marketers is to reach their target customers cost-effectively. Mobile currently works best for younger audiences, but this will change as penetration of smartphones increases among the population as a whole grows.

The advantages of mobile over other media for marketing communications purposes include the following:

- It is personal.
- It goes everywhere with you.
- It is always on (until the battery runs out).
- It is available at the moment of purchase.
- It can be consulted in a flash (no need to boot up).

- It makes bill payments, money transfers and purchases (increasingly 'contactless').
- It transmits metadata of vital importance to marketers.
- It makes large-scale short surveys viable.
- Mobile use is not just about movement of people and goods, but also about information technology of every kind.
- Mobiles are not just about people, but also about communication between machines and devices.

As they did with direct marketing, most traditional advertising agencies (both creative and media) now offer digital marketing services to their clients: at first they acquired or partnered with specialist digital agencies (for example, SEO, email, mobile or content), then they started to build their own resource, either as a stand-alone subsidiary or as a part of the main agency. All the big agencies need to offer digital services given digital's growing share of marketing budgets as marketers integrate it into brands' promotional strategies.

ACTIVITY 6.3

Should we adapt everything to suit local needs and tastes, or go for a standardised approach to our internal and external communication? The product or service on offer will quite possibly be standardised (eg McDonald's, KFC), so should we not standardise our marketing approach too?

REAL LIFE 6.2

McDonald's Canada

The world's leading fast food retailer ran a brave campaign in one country only, entitled 'Our food: your questions'. McDonald's Canada invited customers and potential customers, even the most hostile, 'behind the counter' to look into the kitchens and even to understand the McDonald's supply chain. In an integrated campaign driven by social media, McDonald's invited customers to ask any question about their food, their cooking techniques and indeed about the entire company and answered them publicly in the spirit of transparency and myth-busting.

https://www.youtube.com/watch?v=MBm8145-wp4

The results included the following:

- McDonald's answered over 20,000 questions.
- There were over 14 million video views.
- McDonald's saw dramatic improvements in scores for brand trust and perceptions of quality.

ACTIVITY 6.4

Do you believe that McDonald's genuinely has nothing to hide, so that total brand transparency is a valid strategy for them? Why do you think McDonald's hasn't run this campaign in more countries?

After planning comes implementation, and tools such as Gantt charts can help. Gantt charts, commonly used in project management, are one of the most popular and useful ways of showing activities (tasks or events) displayed against time.

153

6.3

THE LINK BETWEEN INTERNAL AND EXTERNAL COMMUNICATIONS

It's easy to think about an organisation as a faceless entity, when in fact it is made up of people (the seventh P of the extended marketing mix). An organisation's success depends on its 'human resources' – or internal stakeholders – making things happen. It is people, not organisations, who establish and sustain the all-important relationships with external stakeholders. Most employees, including those in marketing, don't come into direct contact with customers, but it is the job of internal marketing to ensure that customers are always at the front of everyone's mind.

Poor or half-hearted internal communication is the biggest barrier to integrated marketing communications. People may feel, for example, that campaigns are too complex to achieve, and office politics, petty power struggles and hidden agendas often thwart the best-laid plans.

We discussed internal marketing and cross-functional relationships in Chapters 1 and 2 of this study guide. But let's briefly recap.

There are two key aspects to internal marketing.

1. The way staff work together across functional boundaries in a way that is aligned with the company's mission, strategy and goals.
2. Everyone in the organisation is both a supplier and a customer. (Christopher *et al* 1991).

Christopher *et al* (2002) suggest a way of segmenting internal customers, according to their proximity with external customers:

- **Contactors** – Have frequent or regular contact with customers and are typically heavily involved with conventional marketing activities (sales or customer service staff, for example).
- **Modifiers** – Are not directly involved with conventional marketing activities, but still have frequent contact with customers (receptionists, switchboard, the accounts department, for example).
- **Influencers** – Are involved with the traditional elements of marketing, but have little or no direct customer contact (product development or market research, for example).
- **Isolateds** – Are support functions that have neither direct customer contact nor marketing input, but whose activities nevertheless affect the organisation's performance (purchasing, HR and data processing, for example).

Internal communications at British Red Cross

When British Red Cross launched a new corporate strategy, it worked hard to bring it to life for its 4,000 staff and 26,000 volunteers - a wide range of people with diverse lives. The internal communications team wanted it to resonate with them on a very personal level so that they would fully engage with it. In essence, they wanted people to think about what they could give back to the busienss to make the strategy work.

The communication needed to be simple and involve staff from the outset, so they began by condensing a 150-page document into a strategy road map with one central vision. They communicated this in six different formats, including video, posters and flyers. The charity already had a digital portal, but it was complicated, so the comms team simplified this too. Then they created what they called 'Meeting in a box' - four one-hour sessions that team leaders could adapt for their respective audiences. It allowed them to ask people what the strategy meant to them, and how they would contribute.

Because people were given the tools and authority to run with their own ideas, and the means to share their experiences with others through the simplified digital portal, the comms team got a very positive response. At the last count, 96% of staff are aware of and understand the aims and objectives of the new corporate strategy and 94% understood how they could contribute.

For another example - the Sovini Group, winner of this year's CIPR internal communications campaign awards, look at the following link.

https://www.cipr.co.uk/sites/default/files/The%20Sovini%20Group_2.pdf

6.4 MEASURING THE EFFECTIVENESS OF INTEGRATED MARKETING COMMUNICATIONS

For any promotion to be successful, it needs to be:

*   well planned and executed.
*   part of an effective integrated promotional mix.
*   consistent with the values and mission of the organisation.

When attempting to measure effectiveness, we should bear in mind three things:

*   Are our customers' needs being satisfied?
*   How competitive is our chosen market?
*   What external factors are affecting us?

Marketing research can help with all these questions. In fact, a developed system of market sensing and a comprehensive marketing information system (MKIS) is needed to constantly evaluate both the marketing effort and IMC campaigns.

The old adage "I know that half of my advertising is wasted; I just don't know which half" may not be quite as true as it used to be given the wealth of measurement tools and techniques that have grown up around marketing. Promotion is probably the single biggest expenditure the organisation makes, so, however difficult it is, marketers have to at least try to measure its success.

Here are some possible tools for measuring different aspects of promotion:

*   Personal selling – sales revenue increases/sales targets met.
*   Public relations – editorial coverage.
*   Direct marketing – enquiries generated.
*   Advertising – brand awareness.
*   Sales promotion – coupons redeemed.
*   Exhibitions – contacts made.

Other more general techniques include the following:

*   Amount and value of attention gained.
*   Communication of defined message.
*   Attitudes improved or modified.
*   Liking for message and execution.
*   Product preference.

Let's look in more detail at how to evaluate each element of the promotional mix.

TV advertising – This is possibly the easiest to assess, as it is the most audited of all media. Comprehensive audience figures are available on a daily basis, at a very detailed level of analysis. The interactivity afforded by digital television allows us to measure audience response by the number of clicks on the 'red button'. Television can also be used in a direct marketing sense by including website addresses and telephone numbers. The difficulty, of course, is gauging the effect TV advertising is having, particularly when viewers are increasingly recording programmes to watch later, or watching them in 'catch-up' mode, both of which typically mean they fast-forward through the adverts.

PR – The traditional measures of column inches or 'advertising value equivalents' can be skewed and possibly irrelevant. Is any publicity good publicity, for example? Studies tracking specific communication to defined target audiences seem much more appropriate.

Sales promotion – Market research can use qualitative methods to assess the relative appeal of different potential promotions and their likely effect on brand image. You can pre-test to ascertain possible redemption levels of coupons in simulated purchasing environments, test stores, area tests and so on. You can also use consumer and retail panels to monitor the results of promotional activity.

Direct marketing – Concepts can be pre-tested here too. And you can use research to follow up reactions to mailing programmes.

Personal selling – All sales can be evaluated by:

- sales achieved (volume/value).
- customer profitability.
- prospects contacted.
- new customer acquisition.
- customer satisfaction.
- new geographic areas opened up.

Using market research to evaluate communication effectiveness

You can use tracking studies to monitor responses over a given period of time. These may be done through surveys or panel research and can include the following:

- Website traffic monitoring.
- Inquiry tests – comparing different campaigns or media.
- Recall and recognition tests – asking consumers if they remember or recognise an aspect of an organisations message. This can be prompted or unprompted.
- Relationship duration – from the organisation's CRM system.
- Retention rate.
- Defection rate.

Measuring the effectiveness of digital marketing

An effective website is highly interactive and serves the customer's needs promptly through rapid, intuitive navigation. Websites are attractive communications media for marketers because of their low cost, their limitlessness and the fact that web analytics deliver comprehensive and detailed viewing statistics.

There are two principal ways to collect information: web server logs and page tagging.

Web server logs – When your web server receives a request it stores details in its server access logs. What it records depends on what you want it to record and the way you set the server up. Ryan and Jones (2013) tell us that the server log file typically contains the following elements:

- The unique IP address of the customer.
- A timestamp showing the date and time of access.
- A status code confirming the result of the request.
- The URL of the page the request came from.
- Other information such as language and operating system.

Page tagging – A small piece of code can be placed on every page of your site that you want to track. When a visitor requests the page, the code sends the information to your chosen provider. The concept of 'software as a service' (SaaS) means that companies like Statcounter (www.statcounter.com) or Google Analytics (www.google.com/analytics) can collect the data and provide the website owner with a wealth of easily-accessible and highly-configurable information.

Many websites and third-party tracking services use http cookies to identify individual users, and this can provide lots of extra information. As we noted earlier (section 5.3), since May 2011 any cookie not considered essential to the functioning of the website must have the visitor's explicit consent to it being placed on the user's device. There is currently much uncertainty around the whole topic of cookies, but new rules proposed by the EU look set to harmonise custom and practice (for example, on the wording of opt in/out clauses on websites) throughout member states, and will make it easier for users to allow or refuse cookies.

Non-EU learners will need to check out the relevant law in their own countries. The overall principle is that users should know what cookies are being placed on their machines, by whom and why, and that they should have the opportunity to decline them.

Financial analysis

Finance is, of course, the language of business, so profitability, marketing expenditure against the budget and ROI are the ultimate measures of the effectiveness of both internal and external communications. However, changes in sales and customer responsiveness may be attributed to a number of different factors, making it difficult to isolate the effect of marketing communications. Over time though, you can allow for some of these other influencing factors, making it easier to come up with a reasonably realistic measurement.

REAL LIFE 6.4

Nivea Brazil – protection campaign
The Nivea brand has always been about protection. The Nivea Kids range helps parents to protect their children's sensitive skin from sun damage. However this campaign took the idea of protection in a different direction – safeguarding children on a crowded beach.

https://www.youtube.com/watch?v=XpRgBt_tbPQ

This campaign combined mobile and offline (magazine) marketing. It was clearly 100% on brand and driven by a clever technical idea (the tag around the child's wrist and the app on the parent's phone), and it has won many awards, both in Brazil and internationally. However some have criticised it as little more than an expensive PR stunt, designed to grab coverage off-line and online.

ACTIVITY 6.5

What can be measured in this campaign?

What can't be measured?

If we can't measure some elements does that mean we shouldn't do them?

Is there anything wrong with doing a PR stunt, particularly if YouTube helps to spread it more widely?

How do you think analytics and measurement in integrated marketing will be improved in future years?

AND FINALLY...

Marketers must never forget that it is the customers who sustain any brand. All communication must be relevant, useful and delivered where and when customers need it, not where and when is most convenient for the organisation. A good example of this is email marketing, where factors including subject line, sender name, content and even time of day can make a crucial difference to 'open' and 'click-through' rates.

Another feature of modern integrated marketing communications is that the interactivity afforded by digital media is blurring the line between marketing and customer service. Brands receive a growing number of customer complaints and queries via Twitter, which means that marketing and customer service have to work more closely together to provide a joined-up service.

REAL LIFE 6.5

Improving customer experience lifts sales
According to Gartner's 2016-2017 CMO Spend Survey, customer experience is the top area of innovation being pursued by marketing leaders. Gartner says that marketing leaders, empowered with larger budgets and spend directed towards innovation efforts, are using analytics to determine the extent to which investments in customer experience pay off. They are using tools such as voice of customer (VoC) surveys alongside customer journey analytics to evaluate the customer experience across different touchpoints and over time.

Gartner cites the example of McDonald's, which reversed a slump in growth and decline in customer numbers a few years ago by using VoC surveys, which showed, among other things, that customers wanted breakfast during lunch and dinner hours, not just at 'breakfast time'. The 'all-day breakfast' menu yielded a 5.7% rise in sales in the quarter after it was launched.

Research shows that a typical business hears from just 4% of its dissatisfied customers. Rather than assuming that all your customers are happy, and then being surprised when they defect to a competitor, wouldn't it make more sense to find out what they really think, and adapt your brand and brand communications accordingly?

QUICK QUIZ – CHECK YOUR KNOWLEDGE

Questions

1. Which is the correct sequence?
   a. Organisational mission statement/functional objectives/ corporate objectives.
   b. Corporate objectives/functional objectives/marketing communications objectives.
   c. Functional objectives/corporate objectives/marketing communications objectives.
2. What is the AC^2ID test (Balmer and Soenen)?
3. According to Fill, what are the 3Ps of promotional strategy?
4. Name six possible reasons for the rise of mobile marketing.
5. Think of six different promotional tools. How can they be measured in terms of effectiveness?
6. How can we use tracking studies to evaluate the effect of a campaign?

Answers

1. b.
2. It examines the different dimensions of corporate identity:
   - Actual identity.
   - Communicated identity.
   - Conceived identity.
   - Ideal identity.
   - Desired identity.
3. Pull, Push and Profiling.
4. Personal, goes everywhere, always on, available at the moment of purchase, can be consulted in a flash, makes bill payments, money transfers and purchases, transmits important metadata, makes large-scale short surveys viable. Mobile use is not just about movement of people and goods, but also about information technology of every kind, including communication between machines and devices.
5. a. Personal selling – sales revenue increases/sales targets met.
   b. Public relations – editorial coverage.
   c. Direct marketing – enquiries generated.
   d. Advertising – brand awareness.
   e. Sales promotion – coupons redeemed.
   f. Exhibitions – contacts made.
6. Tracking studies may be implemented to monitor responses over a period, either through surveys or panel research, and can include:
   a. Website traffic monitoring.
   b. Inquiry tests – comparing different campaigns or media.
   c. Recall tests.
   d. Recognition tests.
   e. Relationship duration.
   f. Retention rate.
   g. Defection rate.

FURTHER READING

Fill, C. and Turnbull, S. (2016) *Marketing communications: discovery, creation and conversations*. 7th edition. Harlow, Pearson. ISBN 9781292092614. Chapters 5–10 pp147–351.

References

Anon (n.d.) What is IMC? Journal of Integrated Marketing Communications.

Anon (n.d.) Internal communications campaign. Sovini Group. https://www.cipr.co.uk/sites/default/files/The%20Sovini%20Group_2.pdf

Anon (2016) IOIC Live conference: the best bits – British Red Cross. May. Synergy. http://www.synergycreative.co.uk/images/7576_IoIC_Live_2016_Conference_Notes.pdf

Anon (2016) Integrated communication campaigns to support citizen behaviour change: a practical guide. WPP. https://www.wpp.com/govtpractice/reports/integrated-comms-behaviour-change/

Balmer, J. M. T. (2001) *From the pentagon: A new identity framework*. Corporate Reputation Review, Vol4(1), pp11–22.

Christopher, M. et al (1991) *Relationship marketing: Bringing quality, customer service and marketing together*. Oxford, Butterworth-Heinemann.

Christopher, M., Payne, A. and Ballantyne, D. (2002) *Relationship marketing: creating stakeholder value*. Abingdon, Routledge.

Fill, C. (2009) *Marketing communications: Interactivity, communities and content*. 5th edition. Harlow, Financial Times/Prentice Hall.

Fill, C. (2013) *Marketing communications: brands, experiences and participation*. 6th edition. Harlow, Pearson.

Fombrun, C. J. (1996) *Reputation: Realizing value from the corporate image*. Boston, Harvard Business School Press.

Gartner CMO Spend Survey 2016–2017 http://gartnerformarketers.com/marketing-spend?rv=cmo-survey&cm_mmc=swg-_-gml-_-mmgmt-_-20161130spe (Registration required)

Infographic http://www.gartner.com/smarterwithgartner/gartner-cmo-spend-survey-2016-2017-infographic/

McKay, E. S. (1972) *The marketing mystique*. New York, American Management Association.

Ryan, D. and Jones, C. (2012) *Understanding digital marketing: Marketing strategies for engaging the digital generation*. Second edition. London, Kogan Page.

van Riel, C. B. M. and Fombrun, C. J. (2007) *Essentials of corporate communication*. Abingdon, Routledge.

YouTube

McDonald's – our food. Your questions. (2013) YouTube, added by DDB Worldwide. https://www.youtube.com/watch?v=MBm8145-wp4

"The protection ad" by Nivea (2014) YouTube, 23 October, Markedu https://www.youtube.com/watch?v=nZ532wkhHYs

Coca-Cola small world machines – bringing India & Pakistan together (2013) YouTube, 19 May, Coca-Cola https://youtu.be/ts_4vOUDImE

163

FEEDBACK TO ACTIVITIES

CHAPTER 1

Activity 1.1

Make a list of all the environmental distractions you can think of that could affect someone's ability to listen to and understand a radio ad for a carpet warehouse.

Feedback to Activity 1.1

It depends where they are when they hear it, but distractions might include the following:

- **At home** – Family members want to chat; the telephone rings; the kettle boils, etc.
- **In the car** – They might need to stop for petrol; they have to negotiate road works or heavy traffic; their phone rings; they meet an ambulance by the roadside, etc.
- **At work** – Their manager comes along to hand out some reports; a colleague requires information; the phone rings, etc.
- **Lack of interest** – The simple fact that 'carpets' will only be a trigger at certain times for most people means most will immediately 'shut off' when they hear the ad.

Activity 1.2

Make a list of the connected stakeholders of your organisation. Are they all equally important to the organisation? Rank or score them in terms of the power and influence each has over the outcomes of the organisation's activities. How important is each one? Now consider your internal stakeholders. What are their respective functions? Do they all contribute equally towards achieving the organisation's objectives?

Feedback to Activity 1.2

This will depend on the nature of your organisation. Connected stakeholders are those with some contractual relationship with the organisation. It would be strange if 'customers' weren't at the top of your list, but it is possible to imagine a 'sellers' market', where people can't get enough of your products and you are short of stock. In this case your supplier is going to be pretty important.

Internal stakeholders won't all have an equal effect on attaining organisational objectives.

Activity 1.3

What communication tools are currently used to communicate with staff in your organisation? How are they used and how could they be used better? Conduct some informal research among your colleagues to see what they think of current methods and their effectiveness.

Feedback to Activity 1.3
Perhaps you can add others to the list that are more creative?
Does current communication not only inform but also inspire employees with the organisational vision and encourage participation and empowerment?

CHAPTER 2

Activity 2.1
As we've seen, there is a strong case for appointing one person to oversee all the organisation's communication. This will ensure a consistent flow of messages, both internally and externally, which will enhance the company's reputation and consolidate its competitive edge. Imagine that you have been asked to prepare an advertisement for a communication manager: describe the skills you would look for.

Feedback to Activity 2.1
The communication manager would need to be an enthusiastic 'people person', coming from an advertising background (commercial side) with an intimate knowledge of media. Digital skills, including social media skills, are essential. Depending on your organisation, the industry and the level of competitive rivalry, specific skills will be needed.

Activity 2.2
Financial forecasting is at the heart of marketing planning. How is budgeting carried out in your company? Explain the processes used, the frequency and timescale of financial plans and the human resource involved. How could it be improved?

Feedback to Activity 2.2
Many organisations simply carry on doing what they always have and applying a typical percentage of sales. The objective and task method is preferable.

Activity 2.3
When it comes to personal skills and practical capabilities, you should consider mapping these against the Professional Marketing Competencies (https://www.cim.co.uk/more/professional-marketing-competencies/). Where you identify a skill or capability gap, think about what experience you could gain in order to plug it. You could ask to be included on a project, for example, or volunteer to help a charity or not-for-profit organisation with a project.

Feedback to Activity 2.3

More information on how to develop your personal skills and practical capabilities can be found on the Professional Marketing Competencies link on the previous page where you will be able to download a PDF.

CHAPTER 3

Activity 3.1

What ads have you seen recently (in any medium) that particularly affected you? Why was each one effective? Would you tend to favour that brand when you are in the market for that particular product category?

For inspiration look here: http://adsoftheworld.com/.

Feedback to Activity 3.1

With this being a personal experience, the feedback is based on that experience and purchasing behaviour. However a planned approach can be taken to analysing behaviour by considering all the factors that influence purchasing and how they apply for a given product or service.

Consider how the decisions on massage framing have been made in relation to:

- Involvement.
- Perceived risk.
- Emotional/rational decision-making.
- Purchase decision-making process.
- Strong and weak theories.

Activity 3.2

We face a dilemma when briefing an advertising agency or design studio: do we give them all the data we have on a product, even negative aspects? Or is it better to keep some things confidential? Will the agency 'leak' details of what we are planning?

Feedback to Activity 3.2

You should provide all research data and management control information to the agency, or they won't be able to conceive the right messages. If you are worried about confidentiality aspects, then choose an agency that can keep its own counsel.

Activity 3.3

Is it safe or responsible to be encouraging drowsy motorists to get behind the wheel, confident that their Café Amazon app will ensure they avoid an accident? Would this campaign be legal in all countries?

Feedback to Activity 3.3

This content may be rejected by some regulatory bodies within countries across the globe. The ethical argument always needs to be considered regardless. It should be realised that this promise cannot be fulfilled given the range of individual circumstances that may occur.

CHAPTER 4

Activity 4.1

Distinguish between brand vision and brand image.

Feedback to Activity 4.1

Brand vision is the way a company seeks to identify, or position, its brands. Brand image is about perception and brand personality and the way the target group understands the brand.

Activity 4.2

Calculate the relative market share for each product/brand of your organisation.

Feedback to Activity 4.2

You calculate relative market share by dividing a brand's share of market (SOM) by the SOM of its largest competitor. If your SOM is 20% and the market leader is 40%, relative market share is 0.5%. In the SME market figures are not readily available so you will need to make a more arbitrary judgement. However it should also be noted that a very newsworthy campaign can create more noise than perhaps expenditure would account for.

CHAPTER 5

Activity 5.1

In September 2014, the Scots went to the polls to vote on whether their country should remain part of the United Kingdom. For many, it seems, the antidote to the global misery that followed the 2007/2008 banking crisis in the West is to 'think smaller and think local'. On the other hand, big multinational corporations want to be seen as your friendly 'local shop'. Even charities, like British Heart Foundation, for example, are trying to create more of a local flavour with their fundraising, to counter perceptions of 'big, faceless, corporate' charities. HSBC dropped its 'world's local bank' positioning several years ago, but McDonald's manages the balance well.

See http://www.global-strategy.net/how-do-you-balance-global-and-local/

Discuss this in class or, if you're studying alone, outline your thoughts on 'global versus local' and potential strategies for different product categories.

For more examples of how be 'glocal', follow these links:

https://www.ama.org/publications/MarketingNews/Pages/achieving-glocal-success.aspx

https://www.forbes.com/sites/sylviavorhausersmith/2012/06/22/cultural-homogeneity-is-not-an-automatic-by-product-of-globalization/#582b3d635034

http://www.shortpress.com.au/why-your-brand-needs-a-glocal-strategy-and-its-not-just-a-buzzword

Feedback to Activity 5.1
The adaptation/standardisation decision across global markets is dependent upon where that market is within the product's life cycle, and the cultural fit between product and consumer. Some products have a natural fit globally whereas others need to be adapted more closely to meet the needs of differing customers.

A standardised approach should be easy when marketing crisps, however PepsiCo crisps are branded under the Walkers name in the UK which maximises the heritage effect in that sizable market, whereas to the rest of the world they are known as Lays.

Activity 5.2
Imagine your line manager is rather conservative when it comes to digital marketing and complains of 'the difficulty in assessing the benefits'. You are preparing for a meeting in which you know you will need to push for further digital activity and greater web presence for your organisation. How will you make your case?

Feedback to Activity 5.2
You could put forward many arguments. Consider the following quote: "Imagine if you could tell not just how many people were visiting your website (your traffic), but for each individual visitor... where they came from (both on the internet and geographically)... what keywords they used to find your site, on which search engine, the page they arrived at, how long they stayed for, what pages they visited ...which page they left from, whether or not they came back again.... Well, the good news is that with modern website and analytics software, you can track all of that information and more". (*Ryan and Jones*, 2013).

Digital marketing excels in providing information on your customers: web analytics can give marketers all the data they need in a timely fashion, based on the information customers themselves provide when they visit the site.

The key challenge for marketers is to analyse intelligently the increasing mass of data on customers and potential customers in order to generate actionable insights. It can be difficult to 'see the wood for the trees' – that is, measure (only) what matters and then use the insights derived to improve marketing effectiveness. The key objective is always to maximise ROI on marketing spend. Specialists in this field are known as data analysts (or data scientists) and their role will become increasingly important within brand-owning companies and their agencies.

CHAPTER 6

Activity 6.1
Coca-Cola has always embraced the brand value of 'happiness' and the concept of sharing good times with people we like. A controversial example of this in practice was the 'Small World machines' campaign. See https://youtu.be/ts_4vOUDImE.

Was Coca-Cola trying to bring the people of Indian and Pakistan together for the genuine benefit of both countries? Or just trying to sell more soft drinks? Is it possible and acceptable to do both?

Feedback to Activity 6.1
What is for sure, is that the technology (combining long-distance communication and drinks vending) served the idea of 'sharing' and portrayed Coca-Cola as a modern brand, appealing to tech-savvy youth (in all countries). Also, the concept was 100% on brand.

Can promoting happiness and uniting people across borders – even when associated with a brand name – ever be a bad thing?

Activity 6.2
At the heart of the organisation is its *raison d'être* (why it is in business), often expressed through its mission statement. Can you relate your own organisation's mission statement to its expressed objectives? Can you distinguish (generally) between objectives, aims, goals, targets and so on? Are these terms synonymous, or does each have a distinct meaning?

Feedback to Activity 6.2
Aims, goals and objectives are confusing terms in business and are often used interchangeably. To help differentiate them, consider these two definitions:

"Aims, unlike objectives, cannot be pursued and measured directly." Noddings, 2007).

"Educational theorists usually think of aims, goals and objectives as descending orders of generality." (Noddings, 2007).

Starting from the **mission statement** and cascading down, what the organisation wishes to achieve can be expressed through: **vision**, corporate **aims** (the most generally stated **purpose**), and strategic (policy) **goals**, followed by marketing and other business **objectives**. This may be rather too arbitrary and hierarchically ordered for some, but it does seem convenient to think in those terms.

Activity 6.3

Should we adapt everything to suit local needs and tastes, or go for a standardised approach to our internal and external communication? The product or service on offer will quite possibly be standardised (eg McDonald's, KFC), so should we not standardise our marketing approach too?

Feedback to Activity 6.3

Religious values, gender roles, etiquette, status (subordinates/ superiors), pace of life and so on are likely to be different in different countries. There will also be differences in infrastructures and technology, business norms and customs, negotiating and decision-making styles and the ways teams function.

You have to bear these things in mind when communicating your product or service. You also have to bear in mind the fact that local competitors don't sit idly by and let you take their customers away. Think about possible competitive responses.

Activity 6.4

Do you believe that McDonald's genuinely has nothing to hide, so that total brand transparency is a valid strategy for them? Why do you think McDonald's hasn't run this campaign in more countries?

Feedback to Activity 6.4

This depends on the regulatory and cultural practices in different countries. However inviting people in to previously 'no access' areas does suggest there is nothing to hide. Across the globe legislations regarding food hygiene will differ, and customer expectations will be different as a result.

This campaign could be misinterpreted as McDonalds solving a problem that didn't exist in some customers minds.

Activity 6.5

What can be measured in Nivea Brazil safety campaign? What can't be measured? If we can't measure some elements does that mean we shouldn't do them? Is there anything wrong with doing a PR stunt, particularly if YouTube helps to spread it more widely? How do you think analytics and measurement in integrated marketing will be improved in future years?

Feedback to Activity 6.5.

Use of digital media and integration of digital techniques into traditional media will undoubtedly aid measurement in the future. In the past Nivea would only have been able to measure how many people saw this ad. Now they can track how many armbands have been activated which gives a more accurate reading of how effective the message is. However, is tracking children always meant as a safety precaution?

The reassurance that children will be safe whilst parents relax is a powerful message. Notice that all of the parents depicted in the ad are on their own. Does this reflect differing needs for security for one parent working families which are on the rise in many countries.

171